Studies in German Literature, Linguistics, and Culture:
Literary Criticism in Perspective

About *Literary Criticism in Perspective*

Books in the series *Literary Criticism in Perspective*, a subseries of the series
Studies in German Literature, Linguistics, and Culture, and *Studies in English
and American Literature, Linguistics, and Culture*, trace literary scholarship and
criticism on major and neglected writers alike, or on a single major work, a
group of writers, a literary school or movement. In so doing the authors —
authorities on the topic in question who are also well-versed in the principles
and history of literary criticism — address a readership consisting of scholars,
students of literature at the graduate and undergraduate level, and the general
reader. One of the primary purposes of the series is to illuminate the nature
of literary criticism itself, to gauge the influence of social and historic currents
on aesthetic judgments once thought objective and normative.

Todd Kontje

The German Bildungsroman: History of a National Genre

CAMDEN HOUSE

Published by Camden House, Inc.
Drawer 2025
Columbia, SC 29202 USA

Printed on acid-free paper.
Binding materials are chosen for strength and
durability.

ISBN:1-879751-53-4

Library of Congress Cataloging-in-Publication Data

Kontje, Todd Curtis, 1954-
    The German Bildungsroman : history of a national genre / Todd Kontje. -- 1st ed.
        p.   cm.   -- (Studies in German literature, linguistics, and culture. Literary
criticism in perspective)
        Includes bibliographical references and index.
        ISBN 1-879751-53-4 (acid-free paper)
        1. Bildungsroman. 2. German fiction--History and criticism.
I. Title. II. Series.
PT747.E6K63   1993
833.009--dc20   93-11688
                                                                          CIP

Contents

Preface

Like *Weltanschauung*, *Weltschmerz*, and *Zeitgeist*, the term *Bildungsroman*
has made its way untranslated into the critical vocabulary of English. *Novel
of development*, *novel of formation*, or *novel of education* could serve as a
rough approximation of the German; but more often than not, English-speaking critics retain the original, frequently uncapitalized and unitalicized. In
doing so, they acknowledge that the genre arose in German-speaking countries both in theory and in practice. Unfortunately, those with no knowledge
of German may know little else about the history of the genre in its native
land. They may not realize, for instance, that postwar critics of German
literature have waged a sustained campaign against the Bildungsroman,
questioning first the term's applicability to particular novels, and, increasingly, the validity of the genre as a whole. Nevertheless, the number of publications about the seemingly moribund genre has soared in recent years. Contri-
butors range from those who seek to sound the final death knell of the German Bildungsroman to others who affix the foreign label to a bewildering
range of homegrown products (Sammons 1991).

This book provides a historical overview of Bildungsroman criticism from
the late eighteenth century to the present, primarily for scholars of the German novel, but also for those who introduce the term into the study of other
national literatures. The criticism on the subject is vast, primarily in German,
and occasionally obscure. Yet it is worth the effort to trace the historical
development of the genre, for contemporary debates about the Bildungsroman
become understandable only in the light of its past. If we begin with a fixed
definition of the genre and set off in search of appropriate examples, we may
well come to conclusion that the Bildungsroman is missing (Sammons 1980).
Yet the genre undoubtedly *does* exist as a topic of critical discussion. Contrary to common critical practice, therefore, I will trace the history of the
Bildungsroman as it has been defined by successive generations of critics. The
focus of the analysis shifts from the literary texts themselves to the critical
discourse about those texts. In short, the following study of the Bildungsroman turns away from the classification of objects and toward the history of
a discourse.

In so doing it participates in a general turn away from the notion that criticism seeks to elucidate the timeless values of acknowledged classics and toward the analysis of the cultural and historical factors that shape the reception of a given text, genre, or author in successive generations of readers. This paradigm shift in the character of literary interpretation has its roots in the reception theory that swept Germany in the wake of 1968, and it continues in current debates about academic standards and the literary canon. The approach proves particularly suitable for an analysis of the Bildungsroman. From its beginnings in the late eighteenth century, the history of the genre has been closely tied to the process of canon formation in German literature, a process which in the nineteenth century contributed to the shaping of a national identity (Hohendahl 1989). Increasingly the Bildungsroman became identified as the quintessentially German genre, one that best expressed alleged national characteristics of inwardness and spirituality. All too often academic analyses of the Bildungsroman became chauvinistic celebrations of German essence, a process that culminated in the fascist appropriation of the genre during the 1930s and 1940s. Much of the current skepticism regarding the German Bildungsroman stems from the suspicion surrounding its history.

Yet not all recent critics have sought to eliminate the Bildungsroman. Feminist criticism offers a particularly interesting example of an attempt to reappropriate the term for the analysis of long neglected authors and works. The interest in the link between gender and genre in the Bildungsroman has also given rise to innovative poststructuralist analyses of canonical works, while the concept of the public sphere offers new perspectives on the place of the Bildungsroman within the institution of literature. Despite protests from within the confines of *Germanistik*, finally, critics from other disciplines continue to employ the term beyond the city gates.

The study is arranged chronologically. Beginning with a brief overview of major eighteenth-century theories of *Bildung*, it then traces the history of the genre from the 1770s to the present. I devote particular attention to the reception of Johann Wolfgang von Goethe's *Wilhelm Meisters Lehrjahre* [Wilhelm Meister's Apprenticeship] (1795-96), as discussions of this novel have played a central role in the development of Bildungsroman theory. Where appropriate I have also included significant studies of other novels that have traditionally been associated with the genre. In reference to the *Lehrjahre* and other works, however, my primary concern lies not in the interpretation of the novels themselves but rather in the role they play in critics' understanding of the genre.

For the sake of convenience I use the term Bildungsroman, capitalized but not italicized, to refer to the genre throughout its history. Those familiar with the genre might well protest that the designation did not gain widespread acceptance until around 1900, and that terminological distinctions between it, the *Entwicklungsroman*, and the *Erziehungsroman* remain unclear. As we shall see, the term itself was in fact used in the early nineteenth century; more important, the critical discussion of the type of novel that gradually became known as the Bildungsroman had already taken its characteristic form in the late eighteenth century. Wilhelminian critics merely adopted a new name for a discourse that was already in place. Attempts to sort out the distinctions between rival terms soon followed, and many more have been introduced since then, including the *Individualroman*, the *Sozialroman*, and the *Identitätsroman*. My concern in the following pages is not to distinguish between the Bildungsroman and the various sub- or alternate genres listed here. Instead, I use the term as an umbrella concept that includes such debates as an integral part of the genre's history.

All references are included parenthetically in the text. For the reader's convenience I have included a list of all works discussed, arranged chronologically according to the date of first publication. A separate chronological list of works cited and an alphabetical index of names follow.

1: *Bildung* and the German Novel (1774-1848)

The belated introduction of the term *Bildungsroman* into the general critical vocabulary requires us to trace two separate strands of thought in writing the history of the genre, namely the concept of *Bildung* and the theory of the novel (*der Roman*). During the last decades of the eighteenth century several prominent German writers began to redefine *Bildung*: the formerly religious term now became a secular humanistic concept. This transformation occurred at a time when the Germans witnessed an astonishing increase in the number of novels published each year. As novel production soared and suspicion of the reading habit grew among church and state authorities, a few critics began to take tentative steps toward granting aesthetic dignity to at least certain types of the modern genre. They did so by singling out two novels that seemed to portray the *Bildung* of the protagonist, Christoph Martin Wieland's *Geschichte des Agathon* [The Story of Agathon] (1766-67) and Goethe's *Wilhelm Meisters Lehrjahre*. Thus the German theory of the novel begins with the appropriation of the concept of *Bildung*. Indeed, much subsequent dissatisfaction with Bildungsroman criticism stems from the fatal first step of substituting a concept of *Bildung* for a close reading of a particular *Roman*.

Theories of *Bildung*

The German word *Bildung* originally referred to both the external form or appearance of an individual (*Gestalt*, Latin *forma*) and to the process of giving form (*Gestaltung, formatio*). Medieval mystics and eighteenth-century Pietists conceived of *Bildung* as God's active transformation of the passive Christian. Through Original Sin humans have fallen out of their unity with God; they have become deformed, *entbildet*. The penitent believer must therefore prepare to receive God's grace. The Catholic believes in the ability to work toward this state of receptivity, whereas the Protestant must rely on faith alone. In the final analysis, however, the believer remains passive in both cases: God impresses His image onto the fallen individual, effecting a redemptive transformation of the disfigured sinner back into the image of God. As the Pietist Gottfried Arnold puts it, "wir müssen zerstöret und entbildet werden, auf daß Christus in uns möge formieret, gebildet werden und allein in uns sein" [we must be destroyed and *entbildet* so that Christ may be formed, *gebildet* within us and be in sole possession of us] (in Vierhaus

1972, 510. On *Bildung* see also Stahl 1934, Lichtenstein 1971, and Cocalis 1978).

This concept of *Bildung* changes significantly in the course of the eighteenth century. Instead of being passive recipients of a preexistent form, individuals now gradually develop their own innate potential through interaction with their environment. Organic imagery of natural growth replaces a model of divine intervention. Transformation into the perfect unity of God turns into the development of one's unique self. In this view, no fall from grace has occurred; humans, like the rest of God's creation, are essentially good. God no longer stands apart from the world but becomes a force of nature — indeed, a part of nature's pantheistic unity. Thus the concept of *Bildung* takes part in the general transformation of Western thought that occurred during the last decades of the eighteenth century. Christian faith in a Second Coming that would mark the end of history yielded to the struggle for human progress in an open-ended process of historical change (see Blumenberg 1966 on the imprecise notion of "secularization").

Johann Gottfried Herder was the most influential disseminator of this new concept of *Bildung*, particularly in his lengthy essay *Auch eine Philosophie der Geschichte zur Bildung der Menschheit* [Also a Philosophy of History on the *Bildung* of Humanity] (1774), followed by the monumental *Ideen zur Philosophie der Geschichte der Menschheit* [Ideas on the Philosophy of the History of Humanity] (1784-91). Herder begins with the primacy of genetics: "Die genetische Kraft ist die Mutter aller Bildungen auf der Erde" [The genetic force is the mother of all life forms on earth] (1784-91, 1: 266). Each individual is unique and born with the genetic material in place. All creatures strive, therefore, to mature into that which they are destined to become. At the same time, external forces affect the development of a given individual or people. Herder refers to these forces with the broad concept of climate (*Klima*), which includes not only the weather and geographical setting in a particular area but also cultural factors such as food and drink, occupation, clothing, habitual posture, and the arts. In describing the effects of climate on indigenous cultures Herder varies the familiar Pietist adage that our lives are merely "clay in the hand of the potter [God]" to argue that we are all "ein bildsamer Ton in der Hand des Klima" [malleable clay in the hand of climate] (1784-91, 1: 261).

For Herder, then, *Bildung* involves the development of innate genetic potential under the influence of a particular geographical and cultural setting. In the *Ideen* he sets out to write nothing less than the history of the world in general and of human civilization in particular. He insists that all human beings are part of the same species, but that different "climates" produce cultural differences between peoples. There is a strong sense of environmental determinism in Herder's work, which leads to a seemingly broad-minded cultural relativism. Thus, he cautions his readers not to condemn past figures on the basis of current standards. Whether we like it or not, they are the inevitable products of a particular time and place (1774, 41). By the same token, Herder claims that he cannot answer the question as to which people in history was the happiest, other than to state that each civilization has its own pinnacle of development. This view of the past also leads to a certain generosity involving present cultural differences, a view that emerges most strikingly in Herder's bitter critique of eighteenth-century colonialism. Europeans have abolished slavery at home only to enslave the world in a misguided attempt to annihilate cultural differences, a practice that contains the seeds of future disaster for Europe (1774, 89, 93, 128-29).

Nevertheless, Herder does not consider all stages of a given culture equal. Like plants and individuals, cultures too have their natural phases of growth, flowering, and decline. Left undisturbed, a culture will eventually attain full maturity. More often than not, however, migration uproots a people from its native soil before it can ripen fully. Just as individual cultures move through an organic cycle, so too humankind as a whole progresses. Already at the pinnacle of creation, it is our duty to move on to an even higher stage. Herder ridicules the notion that humans should devolve into minerals, vegetables, or animals: "soll er [der Mensch] rückwärts gehen und wieder Stein, Pflanze, Elefant werden?" (1784-91, 1: 177-78). Thus Herder overlays his historical determinism and cultural relativism with a teleological narrative that enables him to condemn both past and present cultures, including his own. An improved understanding of the way things necessarily were and are yields to exhortation to his own people to become what they ought to be. This same pedagogical impulse will recur in nineteenth-century discussions of the Bildungsroman, as critics grow impatient with existing literary production and encourage writers to further the progress of the German novel.

The concept of *Bildung* also played a central role in the work of the Weimar Classicists Goethe, Schiller, and Wilhelm von Humboldt. In the first instance, *Bildung* referred to organic growth, the development of the seed to fruit according to innate genetic principles. Goethe took an active interest in the natural sciences and gave his theory of organic development poetic form in "Die Metamorphose der Pflanzen" [The Metamorphosis of Plants] (1799) and "Metamorphose der Tiere" [Metamorphosis of Animals] (1820). Humans also must develop in accordance with their destiny, as he writes in the late poem "Urworte: Orphisch" [Primal Words: Orphic]:

So mußt du sein, dir kannst du nicht entfliehen
So sagten schon Sibyllen, so Propheten;
Und keine Zeit und keine Macht zerstückelt
Geprägte Form, die lebend sich entwickelt.　　(1817, 1: 359)

[As the sibyls and prophets said long ago, that is the way you must
be; you cannot escape yourself. And no time and no power can tear
apart imprinted form that develops in the course of life.]

In his autobiography Goethe stresses the freedom necessary for human development and views personal cultivation as a continuing project of the highest
ethical significance: "Auf eigene moralische Bildung loszuarbeiten, ist das
Einfachste und Tulichste, was der Mensch vornehmen kann" [To go to work
on one's own moral *Bildung* is the simplest and most advisable thing that a
person can do] (1811-14, 10: 88; on the concept of *Bildung* among the
Weimar Classicists see Müller-Seidel 1983).

Humboldt also identifies *Bildung* as the primary goal of humanity in his
Ideen zu einem Versuch die Grenzen der Wirksamkeit des Staats zu bestimmen
[Ideas toward an Attempt to Determine the Limits of State Authority] (1792).
Our true purpose in life is to cultivate our diverse talents into a balanced
whole (1: 106). Humboldt shares Herder's belief in the primacy of genetics
and employs organic metaphors to describe human development. Yet passive
ripening is not good enough for human beings. Nature provides the "seed,"
but it is up to humans to develop to their full potential through active engagement with the world around them. Thus, freedom becomes the first and
essential prerequisite for personal *Bildung*: "Zu dieser Bildung ist Freiheit die
erste, und unerlassliche Bedingung" (1: 106).

Schiller shares Humboldt's belief in the human ability to shape destiny.
In one of his earliest theoretical writings he argues against Johann Kaspar
Lavater's concept of physiognomy, which was based on the belief that one's
physical features determine one's moral character. Schiller insists that the free
intellect impresses its stamp on an individual's outer form, and not vice versa:
"In diesem Verstande also kann man sagen, die Seele bildet den Körper" [In
this sense we can say that the soul shapes the body] (1780, 5: 318). For the
animal, *Bildung* is simply what nature makes it, whereas human freedom
turns *Bildung* into an achievement of the will (5: 454). In his major theoretical works Schiller maintains his belief in the importance of freedom but seeks
an equilibrium between ethical demands and physical needs as the goal of
human *Bildung*. In his view, the ancient Greeks came closest to attaining this
ideal; their achievement stands as an inspiration to the current age, in which
we live in a state of alienation and fragmentation.

The notion of *Bildung* has strong political implications for all three
Weimar Classicists. Each opposes the violence of the French Revolution with
the concept of steady, organic growth.

Was das Luthertum war, ist jetzt das Franztum in diesen
Letzten Tagen, es drängt ruhige Bildung zurück.
(Goethe, "Revolutionen" [Revolutions] 1796, 1: 211)

[In recent days France has become what Lutheranism was; it stifles
tranquil *Bildung*.]

Humboldt begins his *Ideen* by condemning political revolution as unnatural
and goes on to argue that the public interest is best served by a monarchy that
allows individuals to develop freely with a minimum of state intervention
(1792, 1: 129). Finally, Schiller maintains in his *Über die ästhetische
Erziehung des Menschen* [On the Aesthetic Education of Humanity] (1795)
that *Bildung* through art renders political revolution unnecessary. In the ideal
work of art, form and content stand in perfect harmony; contemplation of
such a work reconciles conflicting drives in human beings and thereby completes the *Bildung* of the individual and helps to establish the utopian community of the aesthetic state.

Certain shortcomings in the classical notion of *Bildung* become evident
early on. Schiller formulates his ethical ideal as a true liberation of the individual from rational constraint as body and mind, physical desire and moral
restrictions coexist without conflict. Yet viewed from a more critical perspective, his program of aesthetic education serves as a means to discipline desire
so that one's wishes no longer exceed social limitations. Humboldt also urges
his readers to restrict their endeavors to the narrow sphere in which they are
most competent to act (1796-97, 2: 12). The theme of willful limitation is
already central to Goethe's concept of *Bildung* during the classical period.
"So ist's mit aller Bildung auch beschaffen," writes Goethe in the program-
matic sonnet "Natur und Kunst" [Nature and Art],

Wer Großes will, muß sich zusammenraffen
In der Beschränkung zeigt sich erst der Meister,
Und das Gesetz nur kann uns Freiheit geben.
(1800, 245)

[That's the way it is with all *Bildung*. ... He who seeks greatness must
pull himself together. The master reveals himself first through limitation, and only the law can give us freedom.]

This theme becomes extreme in Goethe's late novel, *Wilhelm Meisters
Wanderjahre* [Wilhelm Meister's Travels] (1821-29). In an encounter with the
character Montan (Jarno in the *Lehrjahre*), Wilhelm Meister makes a feeble
appeal to eighteenth-century optimism, recalling that a many-sided *Bildung*

had once been considered advantageous and necessary. Montan abruptly corrects Meister's outdated views, insisting that now is the time for one-sidedness. In his view, one ought to restrict oneself to the practice of a single trade (37). Slightly later Meister reads a maxim about education that underscores Montan's advice: "'Eines recht wissen und ausüben gibt höhere Bildung als Halbheit im Hundertfältigen'" [To know and practice one thing well yields higher *Bildung* than imperfection in hundreds of things] (148).

Even this compromised ideal was only available to a small percentage of the German population. Schiller published the opening letters of the *Ästhetische Erziehung* as the first contribution to his new literary journal *Die Horen*. In this highly ambitious project Schiller hoped to unite Germany's best writers in working toward the realization of the cultural and political ideals articulated in his theory. The journal did not have the expected success, and Schiller abandoned the project two years later. In the last of his letters on aesthetic education he had already conceded that for the time being, at least, his "aesthetic state" was restricted to a narrow elite ("einigen wenigen auserlesenen Zirkeln" 1795, 669). Precisely this group is of interest for the history of *Bildung* in a social context. Weimar Classicism sought an alliance between progressive members of the nobility and cultivated members of the middle class that cut across traditional social class distinctions determined by birth. In doing so, however, they unintentionally began to split German society along new lines, namely between those who had access to *Bildung* and those who did not. In the course of the nineteenth century *Bildung* would become the exclusive possession of the educated members of the middle class, the *Bildungsbürgertum*, rather than the collective achievement of a unified people (Engelhardt 1986).

A final point worth mentioning in this context concerns the role of gender in classical theories of *Bildung*. Thomas Laqueur has argued that the concept of radical biological differences between men and women emerged for the first time during the late eighteenth century (1990). Not coincidentally, this period witnessed the proliferation of pedagogical treatises concerning the proper way to raise children of different sexes. Rousseau's *Emile* (1762) spawned numerous German tracts on the subject, including a popular work by Wilhelm von Humboldt's childhood tutor Johann Heinrich Campe entitled *Väterliche Rath für meine Tochter* [Fatherly Advice for my Daughter] (1782). Humboldt, in turn, produced two philosophical treatises on the "natural" differences between the sexes: "Über den Geschlechtsunterschied und dessen Einfluß auf die organische Natur" [On Sexual Difference and its Influence on Organic Nature] (1794) and "Über die männliche und weibliche Form" [On Masculine and Feminine Form] (1795). From today's perspective Humboldt's arguments sound like an attempt to place a pseudoscientific veneer on his contemporary cultural prejudices. Thus, he concludes that women are naturally passive, men active; men are rational, women imaginative. He associates the masculine with freedom, while identifying women with nature. In his slightly earlier essay *Über Anmut und Würde* [On Grace and Dignity] (1793), Schiller had written the same cultural stereotypes into his aesthetic theory, ascribing beauty and grace to women while reserving dignity and the sublime for men. Neither Humboldt nor Schiller means to degrade women. Both are delighted by the seemingly natural symmetry between the sexes, and both conceive of a human ideal that would unite the two opposites in one. Yet the way in which they formulate sexual difference effectively precludes the possibility of female development. As both Humboldt and Schiller stress, human freedom is absolutely necessary for personal growth; by equating women with nature, they deny women any chance of participating in the process of *Bildung* (see Bovenschen 1979, 244-56).

Taken together, these eighteenth-century theories of *Bildung* provide much raw material for future studies of the novel. On the surface, the authors profess an optimistic belief in progress for both the individual and society that will carry over to early discussions of the Bildungsroman. Yet the same theories also hint at a less appealing state of affairs in which *Bildung* is a form of social discipline that requires personal resignation, is restricted to a cultural elite, and for men only. The critical backlash against the affirmative interpretation of the Bildungsroman will locate in the novels themselves aspects of the negativity that are already incorporated in the concept of *Bildung*.

The Beginnings of Bildungsroman Theory

Christoph Martin Wieland published the first version of his novel *Die Geschichte des Agathon* in 1766-67. Set in the Mediterranean lands of classical antiquity, it tells of the eponymous hero's eventful life. Throughout the novel Wieland makes ironic use of the sort of escapades the reader might expect to find in a sensational adventure story: within the first five chapters Agathon is abducted by pirates, sold into slavery, and seduced by a famous courtesan. Wieland's primary concern, however, lies in the depiction of his protagonist's psychological growth. We follow Agathon from childhood to maturity as he experiences love, war, and politics. By the end of the novel the youthful enthusiast (*Schwärmer*) has been sobered by life's vicissitudes and goes into retirement.

Within a few years Christian Friedrich von Blanckenburg published his *Versuch über den Roman* [Essay on the Novel] (1774), which is recognized as the first significant German theory of the novel. To be sure, the Prussian officer's five-hundred-page treatise is long-winded and repetitious, and he

takes many of his examples from drama rather than from the novel. Nevertheless, Blanckenburg recognizes that Wieland's *Geschichte des Agathon* is a
new type of novel that deserves to be taken seriously. Blanckenburg goes
further, countering the commonly assumed supremacy of Greek culture and
the notion of historical decline. While the Greeks had their epic, he argues,
the novel is the appropriate genre of the modern age. Thus, Blanckenburg
defends the integrity of his indigenous culture and encourages young writers
to produce a German national classic (xvii-xviii; also 72. On Blanckenburg's
significance, see Lämmert 1965, 575).

Blanckenburg's understanding of his theory as a set of instructions to
young writers, as a sort of literary cookbook, reveals his indebtedness to an
older Enlightenment poetics that stressed craft over innovation, as does his
repeated assertion that all artists should seek to instruct through delight. His
most original comments come in connection with *Agathon*. He claims that
Wieland unifies his novel by portraying Agathon's inner development in strict
accordance with the laws of causality. The ancient epic portrayed "Thaten des
Bürgers," public events, whereas the modern novel focuses on the inner life,
"das Seyn des Menschen, sein innrer Zustand" (17-18). By emphasizing
Wieland's concentration on the psychological development of one central
protagonist, Blanckenburg identifies the beginning of a German novel tradition that will come to be called the Bildungsroman.

Several aspects of Blanckenburg's discussion deserve particular notice.
Blanckenburg is in search of authors who cultivate good taste and better
morals. Thus, he will condemn picaresque novels because they corrupt society
by preventing the spread of "the true, the good, and the beautiful" (307-8).
In holding up Wieland's novel as a salutary counterpart to these salacious
works, however, Blanckenburg remains insensitive to Wieland's irony in the
depiction of his hero. As we shall see, willful blindness to irony will characterize the reception of Goethe's work as well, and indeed, it becomes a
standard feature of much Bildungsroman criticism up to the present day (on
Blanckenburg's lack of irony, see Lämmert 1965, 558).

Blanckenburg's theory of the novel also marks an early stage in what has
been termed the "dichotomization" of German literature, the split between
elite and popular culture (Bürger 1982). Blanckenburg begins by recognizing
the widespread prejudice against the novel as a form of entertainment written
only for the masses. He goes on to claim, however, that two or three novels
— or maybe only one — stand out among the crowd. These exceptional works
deserve to be read differently: whereas the novel of adventure offers entertainment for one fast reading, the superior novel invites repeated study (378).
In making this distinction Blanckenburg is responding to the changing reading
habits of the German public. Rolf Engelsing has argued that former "inten-
sive" rereaders of the Bible became "extensive" consumers of secular fiction

during the last decades of the eighteenth century (1974, 182-215). Whereas earlier readers concentrated on repeated study of a single text, the new readers devoured vast quantities of disposable fiction. In his *Versuch über den Roman*, however, Blanckenburg maintains that certain works of fiction should be studied with the care formerly reserved for religious texts. His work thereby marks the beginning of a consistent pattern in histories of the German novel: the Bildungsroman will become the only form of the novel granted canonical status as the secular scripture of German literature.

The nascent split between the popular novel and a select number of demanding works becomes particularly evident in the reception of Goethe's *Wilhelm Meisters Lehrjahre*. Novel production in Germany had increased dramatically in the thirty years that separate the *Lehrjahre* from *Agathon*, and the reading habit had taken hold in the emerging bourgeois public. Yet most critics continued to consider the novel a minor genre, and voices of authority in the government and the pulpit railed against the moral corruption spawned by the "reading obsession" (*Lesesucht*) or "reading madness" (*Lesewut*). While younger readers contributed to the sensational success of Goethe's *Die Leiden des jungen Werther* [The Sufferings of Young Werther] (1774), members of an older generation soberly condemned its apparent justification of suicide. Some twenty years later Goethe disappointed the expectations of many members of the public again, this time because his new novel lacked the immediate appeal of *Werther*. Yet the disapproval was not universal, as some of Germany's foremost writers celebrated the *Lehrjahre* as the most significant German novel to date. Comments by Friedrich Schiller, Christian Gottfried Körner, Friedrich Schlegel, and Friedrich von Hardenberg (Novalis) are of particular importance in the history of the Bildungsroman. Although they do not yet use the term, their contrasting assessments of Goethe's novel anticipate much of the subsequent discussion of the genre (on the unfavorable reception of the *Lehrjahre* see Gille 1971, 81-82 and Mandelkow 1980, 45).

Goethe had begun his novel in the late 1770s as "Wilhelm Meisters theatralische Sendung" [Wilhelm Meister's Theatrical Mission], and had made halting progress on it in the years before his first trip to Italy in 1786. A copy of this early draft was found in 1910. It depicts a young, middle-class man drawn to the stage both for personal excitement and in the vague hope of establishing a German national theater. In the substantially revised version published a decade later, Goethe reduced Wilhelm Meister's involvement with the theater to a long episode in a larger project of self-cultivation. A group of enlightened aristocrats who comprise the secret *Turmgesellschaft* (Tower Society) watch over Meister without his knowledge. They arrange for his marriage to the noble Natalie just as Meister has begun to despair in his efforts to gain control of his life. The sudden turn of events leaves Meister stunned by his unexpected good fortune as the novel concludes.

The *Lehrjahre* holds a unique place among Goethe's major works in that his correspondence with Schiller grants us a glimpse into the process of composition. From December 1794 until the summer of 1796 Goethe sent Schiller successive stages of the expanding project: first the already typeset opening books, and later the manuscript for the novel's conclusion. Schiller responds with astonished delight to each new delivery, initially offering only cautious suggestions for minor revisions. Increasingly, however, he displays impatience with what he feels is Goethe's unwillingness to express more clearly "die Idee des Ganzen," the single concept that unifies the whole (1794-96, 526). The process culminates in a long letter of July 8, 1796, in which Schiller expresses what he feels is the significance of Wilhelm's development: "Er tritt von einem leeren und unbestimmten Ideal in ein bestimmtes tätiges Leben, aber ohne die idealisierende Kraft dabei einzubüßen" [He steps from an empty and unspecified ideal into a specific active life, but without losing the idealizing energy in the process] (541). Schiller echoes his own aesthetic theory in this assessment of Goethe's hero: Meister moves from what Schiller terms the "leere Unendlichkeit" [empty infinity] of youth in his twenty-first letter on the concept of aesthetic education to the "erfüllte Unendlichkeit" [fulfilled infinity] of his aesthetic and anthropological ideal (1795, 635). Thus, Schiller views *Wilhelm Meisters Lehrjahre* through the lens of his own theory of *Bildung*; the novel's only shortcoming stems from Goethe's reluctance to state its (Schillerian) message more clearly. At this point Goethe politely signals that he is no longer willing to collaborate with Schiller on the project. After responding with a self-deprecating description of the peculiar personality trait (*Tick*) that leads him to ironic understatement (1796a, 543), Goethe sent the manuscript to press without showing it to Schiller again.

While Schiller acknowledged that his own convictions were not expressly formulated in Goethe's text, Körner ignored the discrepancy altogether. Körner developed his interpretation in a lengthy letter to Schiller, who published it with minor revisions in his journal, *Die Horen*. In this letter Körner simply borrows the classical ideal of *Kalokagathie* to characterize Wilhelm Meister's development:

> Die Einheit des Ganzen denke ich mir als die Darstellung einer schönen menschlichen Natur, die sich durch die Zusammenwirkung ihrer inneren Anlagen und äußern Verhältnisse allmählich ausbildet. Das Ziel dieser Ausbildung ist ein vollendetes Gleichgewicht, Harmonie mit Freiheit. (1796, 552)

> [In my opinion the unity of the whole lies in the representation of a beautiful human nature that gradually takes form through the interac-

tion of inner predispositions and external circumstances. The goal of this formation {*Ausbildung*} is a perfect equilibrium, harmony with freedom.]

Like Blanckenburg before him, Körner remains blind to the irony in the text he analyzes. Yet his interpretation was to prove enormously influential throughout the nineteenth and well into the twentieth century both for the interpretation of Goethe's novel and for the definition of the Bildungsroman as genre (see Gille 1971, 5, 37, 41-43).

While Schiller's publication of Körner's letter might suggest approval, he expressed reservations about Körner's approach to the novel in a letter to Goethe of November 28, 1796. In Schiller's view, Körner had exaggerated the importance of Goethe's protagonist while paying insufficient attention to the overall structure of the work. It was just this structure that Friedrich Schlegel highlighted in his lengthy review of Goethe's novel. As he writes, this is not the sort of work whose primary purpose is to portray characters and events. As readers, we may enjoy the individual parts at first, but eventually we learn to appreciate the entire work. In accordance with his own theory of romantic poetry, Schlegel viewed the novel as an example of metafiction, "Poesie der Poesie," an organic whole unified through its self-reflexive structure. Thus, Schlegel was able to view the theoretical discussions about poetry within the novel, in particular the extended interpretation of Shakespeare's *Hamlet*, as an integral part of the whole. In Schlegel's opinion, the very self-critical awareness of Goethe's novel threatens to render further commentary superfluous, since it is one of those books that interpret themselves (133-34; on Schlegel's essay see Eichner 1967 and Gille 1971).

Schlegel's concentration on the novel's structure has an important effect on his understanding of the *Bildung* the work portrays. Unlike Körner, Schlegel argues that Goethe does not depict the *Bildung* of any given individual. In his opinion, it is the natural process of *Bildung* itself compressed into simple, fundamental principles that Goethe illustrates with numerous examples (143). As a result, Schlegel has a keen eye for the irony with which the narrator views Wilhelm's development. "Es sind doch auch Lehrjahre, in denen nichts gelernt wird, als zu existieren" [But they are after all also years of apprenticeship in which nothing is learned other than to exist] (141). As Schlegel views it, the novel ends not with the triumphant maturation of Wilhelm Meister but with his passive acquiescence to the will of the Tower Society: "Er resigniert förmlich darauf, einen eignen Willen zu haben; und nun sind seine Lehrjahre wirklich vollendet, und Nathalie wird Supplement des Romans" [He formally abdicates his own desires, and now his apprenticeship is really over, and Natalie becomes the novel's supplement] (144).

Whether or not Schlegel intended his characterization of Wilhelm Meister as an indirect attack on the novel and its author is a matter of some dispute. From today's perspective, at least, Schlegel's essay clearly anticipates the work of more recent critics who have emphasized the irony in the *Lehrjahre* and in the genre of the Bildungsroman as a whole. More immediately influential were Novalis's biting comments on the novel, published posthumously in edited form by his friend Ludwig Tieck. Actually, the hostility evident in some of Novalis's most frequently cited comments on the *Lehrjahre* obscures the immense significance of the work for his own development as a poet. Novalis treasured Goethe's novel as he did no other literary text. After the death of his beloved Sophie von Kühn he sought comfort and distraction through daily study of *Wilhelm Meisters Lehrjahre*, and his friends report that he knew long passages of the novel by heart. It was only in 1800 that his criticism took a sharp turn to the negative; at this time Novalis was composing his own *Heinrich von Ofterdingen* (1802), which he conceived as both a response to and a rejection of Goethe's work. In our post-Freudian age it is easy enough to ascribe the vehemence of his critique to his need to overcome a powerful influence.

Novalis attacks the novel primarily because it affirms the mundane and seems hostile toward anything mystical, poetic, or romantic: "*Wilhelm Meisters Lehrjahre* sind gewissermaßen durchaus prosaisch und modern. Das Romantische geht darin zugrunde, auch die Naturpoesie, das Wunderbare" (1798-1800, 571). Like Schiller and Schlegel, Novalis measures Goethe's novel against his own conception of poetry and finds it sorely lacking. He laments Goethe's extirpation of the irrational, and places a high value on Mignon and the Harpist in an interpretation that soon proved influential among German romantic novelists (Gille 1971, 173). Novalis also prepared the ground for future political interpretations of the novel with his sharp critique of Wilhelm Meister's entry into the group of nobles who comprise the Tower Society: "*Das Ganze ist ein nobilitierter Roman. Wilhelm Meisters Lehrjahre oder die Wallfahrt nach dem Adelsdiplom*" [The whole thing is an ennobled novel. *Wilhelm Meister's Apprenticeship or the Pilgrimage to the Patent of Nobility*] (1798-1800, 571). One might feel that there is an element of bad faith in this last remark, for not only did Novalis himself come from an old noble family but he also wrote paeans to the Prussian monarch in his collection of fragments entitled *Glaube und Liebe* [Faith and Love] (1798) and created a idealized view of medieval feudalism in the essay "Die Christenheit oder Europa" [Christianity or Europe] (1799). Nevertheless, Novalis staked out an alternative to Körner's position in his uncompromising critique of *Wilhelm Meisters Lehrjahre;* together these two early readers of Goethe's novel established the boundaries for its subsequent discussion and for the theory of the Bildungsroman.

Meanwhile, Novalis and his contemporary Romantics were busy contributing to the practice of the Bildungsroman as well. Even before Novalis completed *Heinrich von Ofterdingen*, Tieck had published *Franz Sternbalds Wanderungen* (1798), the story of a young painter who starts out as Albrecht Dürer's apprentice. In deliberate opposition to Goethe, Tieck sets his novel in an idealized version of Germany at the time of the Reformation. In this decidedly more "romantic" atmosphere his protagonist aspires to artistic greatness throughout the novel — unlike Meister, who turns away from the theater to join the nobility. Novalis goes still further back in time to the Middle Ages for the setting of his novel, which tells of a young man's discovery of his innate talent as a poet. Novalis heightens the poetic effect of his text by incorporating several fairy tales into the narrative, including one of his own invention.

The attempt of these early Romantics to rewrite Goethe's novel in accordance with their own artistic beliefs marks the beginning of a continuing development in the history of the Bildungsroman and its criticism. To a certain extent, the history of the genre coincides with the reception of Goethe's *Lehrjahre,* as successive generations of critics revise their understanding of what soon came to be considered the prototypical Bildungsroman in the light of their own cultural and historical situations. At the same time, however, German writers for the last two hundred years have created works that both extend and revise the literary tradition. These works, in turn, become the subject of critical attempts to reconceive the history of the Bildungsroman. Thus, at least three factors combine to produce the history of the Bildungsroman over time: the changing reception of the old literature, the production of the new, and the effort to situate the new literature in the context of the growing literary tradition.

Liberal Critics and Wilhelm Meister's Legacy

The defeat of Napoleon in 1815 marked the beginning of a sharp turn to the right in German politics. The conservative postwar governments of Prussia and the Austro-Hungarian Empire sought to turn back the clock to the prerevolutionary era. During this same period a rising tide of opposing liberal thought gained momentum and culminated in the short-lived triumph of democracy in the March revolution of 1848. The governments reacted consistently with attempts to suppress dissidence, beginning with the Draconian Carlsbad Decrees of 1819 and continuing with the official ban on the publications of the radical Young Germans in 1835, until the quick collapse of the disorganized Frankfurt Parliament brought the restoration of conservative rule.

The period between 1815 and 1848 was also crucial in shaping the understanding of the novel. Novel production had slumped during the French occupation of Germany and the Wars of Liberation, but the book market quickly resumed the explosive rate of growth that had begun in the last decades of the eighteenth century. Illiteracy decreased, and the novel-reading habit spread into a broader percentage of the population. Yet widespread distrust of the genre as being both aesthetically careless and morally dangerous persisted. Only in the course of the next decades do we witness a gradual shift in the assessment of the novel, until by mid-century it is acknowledged as the representative genre of modernity (Steinecke 1975, ix, 4-7).

Hartmut Steinecke has played a central role in the reevaluation of early nineteenth-century German novel theory. He concedes that the academic aesthetics and poetics after 1815 seem shallow and derivative when compared with the work of the early Romantics. We must look elsewhere when seeking significant contributions to the study of the novel during the period, namely, to publications that are not conceived as aesthetic theory in the narrower sense of the term. These publications include prefaces, newspaper articles, contributions to reference works, and book reviews (1987, 13). Conservative academic critics grew increasingly silent on the subject of the novel in the decades leading up to 1848, for the genre that was already suspect on aesthetic and moral grounds was now perceived as a democratic, hence politically subversive, art form. By the 1840s significant contributions to the understanding of the novel came almost exclusively from critics who were considered politically progressive (1975, 112, 132).

The liberal political agenda of many literary critics during these decades helps explain why they chose to publish their views in newspapers and other publications aimed at a popular audience. One of the major goals of the Young Germans was to bring literature back into contact with life praxis. As Peter Uwe Hohendahl has argued, their strategy entailed a democratization of the public sphere. In the liberal model of the late eighteenth century, literature was part of a public sphere that was theoretically open to all but that was in fact limited to members of the educated middle class. Such critics as Georg Herwegh and Ludwig Börne sought to extend literary discussion to the entire population, thereby making it an agent of political reform. "Accordingly, the locus of literary criticism was not erudite professional conversation or the small circle of the literary coterie but newspapers and journals" (Hohendahl 1989, 119).

The German novel itself underwent significant changes during this period. As early as Joseph Freiherr von Eichendorff's *Ahnung und Gegenwart* [Presentiment and Presence] (1815) we see evidence of a shift away from the early romantic Bildungsroman. In the opening section of this novel Eichendorff rehearses what had become clichés of romantic fiction: his handsome, aristocratic hero Friedrich moves in a springtime world of wine, women, and song. Yet Eichendorff sets his work in the historical present, and the bucolic world soon fades into a bitterly satirical portrait of his contemporary urban salon culture. Friedrich rejects this decadent society to become a heroic soldier in the struggle against Napoleon. In the end he renounces the world entirely and becomes a monk. History has interrupted the idyll: *Ahnung und Gegenwart* evidences a pan-German nationalism and a strict Catholic moralism foreign to the spirit of both the early romantic novel and the *Lehrjahre*.

Social and political satire also play a large role in E. T. A. Hoffmann's considerably less reverent *Lebens-Ansichten des Katers Murr* [The Life and Opinions of Tomcat Murr] (1819-21). The ostensible hero of this Bildungsroman is a genial cat. His autobiography parodies the pretensions of the new social type of the *Bildungsphilister*, who acquires culture as a status symbol. Interspersed by "accident" in Murr's autobiography is the biography of the tormented musician Johannes Kreisler. He is entangled in the intrigues of a ludicrously corrupt provincial court that serves as a metaphor for Metternich's Europe. Meanwhile, Murr suffers persecution for his association with a fraternal feline order in an episode that makes transparent reference to the Prussian government's brutal repression of the *Burschenschaft* [liberal student fraternity] movement. For the liberal Hoffmann the Bildungsroman has become a vehicle for critique of both reactionary politics and social climbing.

European developments in the novel had a particularly strong influence on German writers in the next decades. Walter Scott's historical novels inspired a wealth of German imitations during the 1820s, while the social novels of Honoré Balzac, Georges Sand, and Eugène Sue played an increasingly significant role in German literary discussions of the 1830s and 1840s. Throughout this period, however, German writers and critics remained acutely aware of their own national tradition, and debate centered on the relation between indigenous literary production and foreign influence. The *Lehrjahre* featured prominently in these debates, for whether it was accepted or rejected, its status as the quintessentially *German* novel made it impossible to ignore (Steinecke 1984).

It was common in the literary criticism of the early twentieth century to credit Wilhelm Dilthey with coining the word *Bildungsroman* in his 1870 biography of the theologian Friedrich Schleiermacher until Fritz Martini revealed in 1961 that Karl Morgenstern, an obscure professor of rhetoric at the Prussian university in Dorpat — today Tartu in Estonia — had used the term as early as 1803 and had published three essays on the Bildungsroman between 1817 and 1824. One might, therefore, expect to find in Morgenstern a bold but forgotten precursor of later nineteenth-century thought; but in fact his ideas are thoroughly typical of his own age. At first glance Morgenstern's positions actually appear more anachronistic than innovative. He openly admits his indebtedness to Blanckenburg, and many of his main ideas fall in line with Blanckenburg's Enlightenment optimism. Morgenstern contends that the Bildungsroman focuses primarily on the inner development of the hero and secondarily on the education of the reader:

> *Bildungsroman*, sagten wir, wird er heißen dürfen, 1. und vorzüglich, wegen des Stoffs, weil er des Helden Bildung in ihrem Anfang und Fortgang bis zu einer gewissen Stufe der Vollendung darstellt; 2. aber auch, weil er gerade durch diese Darstellung des Lesers Bildung in weiterm Umfang als jede andere Art des Romans fördert (1824, 74).

> [We said that we may call it the *Bildungsroman*, first, and primarily, on account of its content, because it represents the *Bildung* of the hero in its beginning and progress to a certain stage of completion; but also second, because just this depiction promotes the *Bildung* of the reader more than any other sort of novel.]

It might seem surprising to find Blanckenburg's ideas of the 1770s recurring nearly verbatim some fifty years later. Yet the seemingly decisive turn from Enlightenment didacticism to aesthetic autonomy in the work of Moritz, Kant, and Schiller in the closing decades of the eighteenth century did not affect all spheres of literary production and reception. As Christa Bürger has shown, the Enlightenment tradition continued well into the nineteenth century on a popular level (1982), and Morgenstern's essays bear witness to this continuity.

Yet Morgenstern's work also reveals the influence of his own position in literary history, particularly in the status he confers on *Wilhelm Meisters Lehrjahre*. Although he mentions Wieland's "unforgettable" *Agathon* in passing, he singles out Goethe's novel for special praise. Particularly significant for later definitions of the Bildungsroman is that Morgenstern ignores the irony noted by several of the novel's early critics. Instead, he reiterates Körner's insistence that Meister completes his *Bildung* successfully. That this understanding of the novel had begun to take hold in broad circles becomes evident if we compare Morgenstern's position with the viewpoint represented in Brockhaus's *Conversations-Lexicon* of 1817. The anonymous author of an article on the novel describes the *Lehrjahre* in terms that are identical to Morgenstern's description of the Bildungsroman in everything but name. In this view, the novel depicts the life experiences of a young man from birth to his completed *Bildung*, identified as the point when the apprentice becomes a master (5).

In equating *Wilhelm Meisters Lehrjahre* with the novel, the author of the Brockhaus article deliberately excludes from discussion the vast majority of novels published at the time. Here the holdings of the Castle Corvey Library prove instructive, for the collection offers the most complete survey of German novels published between 1815 and 1830 (Steinecke 1991). The catalogue reveals that historical, comic, Gothic, and adventure novels were by far the most common genres. Wolfgang Menzel confirms this impression in an 1830 survey of the German novel in which he mentions love stories, family histories, and historical novels, but not works written under the immediate influence of the *Lehrjahre*. In short, both Morgenstern and the author of the Brockhaus article encourage an idealized novel form while ignoring or repudiating the bulk of actual literary production. Morgenstern cautions his readers against disreputable novels dashed off by literary hacks and encourages the study of noble works by great writers (1824, 99). In doing so, he widens the gap between serious literature and popular fiction opened by Blanckenburg in his *Versuch über den Roman*. Once again, discussion of the Bildungsroman serves the purpose of legitimating a particular type of German novel at the expense of what most writers wrote and most readers read.

One consequence of the identification of the novelist's subject with the "Lehrjahre des Jüngers" [apprenticeship of the young man] was to relegate fiction by or about women to second-rate status. Morgenstern, for instance, is aware of women writers and even mentions several prominent female authors and their titles in his last essay; but he considers their works examples of the aesthetically inferior *Familienroman* (1824, 93-94). Some years later Karl Menzel will argue that all novels by women are *Entsagungsromane* [novels of resignation] (1830, 77). In an earlier talk, however, delivered — perhaps not coincidentally — soon after the defeat of Napoleon, Morgenstern implies that there is something effeminate about the heroes of the Bildungsroman that limits their effectiveness in inspiring a "männlich-moralische Denkart" [manly-moral way of thinking] among their readers. Such milquetoasts hardly set a proper example for the current age: "Wahrlich; wir leben in einer Zeit, wo Europa der Männer bedarf" [Truly; we live at a time when Europe needs men] (1817, 53-54).

Finally, Morgenstern's moralizing approach to fiction threatens to turn the reading of "good" German novels into a form of self-imposed penance. "*Res severa est verum gaudium,*" cautions Morgenstern sternly, with a reference to Seneca (1824, 99). This theme will recur frequently in twentieth-century Bildungsroman criticism, particularly in works by non-native Germans. In the arts, mere pleasure is suspect; the acquisition of culture requires hard work. Small wonder that the Bildungsroman has attained the double reputation of being Germany's most significant contribution to the history of the novel and the one that is least entertaining to read.

The translation of Walter Scott's *Ivanhoe* into German in 1820 sparked widespread interest in the historical novel throughout the decade. With its focus on a broad panorama of a particular period rather than on the development of a single protagonist, this type of novel stood in direct opposition to the German tradition of the Bildungsroman. Willibald Alexis's 1823 study "The Romances of Walter Scott" offers a good example of the German reception of the historical novel. Alexis views the *Lehrjahre* as the source of a type of German *Kunstroman* [art novel] in which ideas about art or intellectual concerns take precedence over events. Although "the philosophic German" has gotten used to abstract thought in works of art, too many novels have become mere vehicles for sententious aphorisms, producing more boredom than enlightenment. Moreover, such works will never appeal to a broad audience. In effect, Alexis reverses Morgenstern's position: he finds excessive interiority on the part of the protagonist suspect and declares the work's popularity a virtue. (On the incompatibility of the historical novel with the Bildungsroman, see Steinecke 1975, 35.)

Yet Alexis's argument in favor of the historical novel takes a circuitous path *through* the Bildungsroman, rather than setting off in a completely different direction. He begins by asserting that the novel descends from the heroic epic and that the German *Kunstromane* represent a degenerate species of the genre, "nur eine Abart" (22). We cannot, however, simply re-create an ancient epic in modern times. Heroic actions occur rarely today, and the novel records events that are significant in the development of quieter lives. To this extent Alexis remains in agreement with a critical tradition that stretches back to Blanckenburg. At the same time, the depiction of the protagonist's mind is not enough for Alexis; he argues that the highest and most popular work of art will be one that reveals the imprint of the inner life on external reality (*"wo das innere Leben ausgeprägt im äußern,"* 26). The good novelist, in his view, begins with the description of an individual life and proceeds to bring this individual into contact with the surrounding world until the character of the "so-called hero" recedes entirely, leaving us with the objective depiction of external reality: "Dieß scheint uns der Sieg der Objektivität über die Subjektivität und vielleicht die Bestimmung aller Romane" [This appears to us as the victory of objectivity over subjectivity, and perhaps the destiny of all novels] (33). The subjective Bildungsroman becomes an intermediate stage on the way to the production of the modern, objective epic in the form of the historical novel.

As Steinecke points out, the German liberals' embrace of the historical novel reflected a general turning away from idealistic systems and theoretical speculation and toward contemporary reality (1975, 50). The Napoleonic Wars and the Wars of Liberation had brought the Germans into direct contact with events of world-historical significance. As Wolfgang Menzel observed, the Germans had witnessed revolutions, mass emigrations, and great suffering with their own eyes. After such experiences, poets could no longer retreat to the private sphere of the family. In Menzel's view, writers should pay tribute to the spirit of the age by producing historical novels: "Der historische Roman ist mithin das ächte Kind seiner Zeit" [The historical novel is therefore the genuine child of the age] (1827, 59). Menzel adds a political element to his interpretation of Scott's novels when he maintains that they represent the people and are therefore democratic, whereas older tales of heroism reflect the values of the monarchy or aristocracy.

Having declared their allegiance to the historical novel, critics soon began to see *Wilhelm Meisters Lehrjahre* in a different light. The author of the Brockhaus article had declared the *Lehrjahre* the best novel of all time, while noting that there was something peculiarly German in its idealistic concentration on purely personal development. In contrast, liberal critics of the 1820s began to view German inwardness, as reflected in its literature, with more regret than pride. Germany's spiritual triumphs seemed only to mask its political malaise. Contrasting the isolated German writer with the well-traveled Englishman or the socially sophisticated Frenchman, Heinrich Heine concludes that the German has no option but to retreat into an imaginary world: the Germans write novels populated by splendid, exquisitely poetic creatures that unfortunately have no counterpart in reality (1822, 19). In 1825 Ludwig Börne sarcastically suggests that the Germans cannot produce significant novels because they are too much like Wilhelm Meister: passive, complacent, and submissive. "Wir haben keine Geschichte ... keine Freyheit zu sagen, was wir noch mehr nicht haben. Woher Romane?" [We have no history ... no freedom to say all those other things we lack. Whence novels?] (36).

The Young Germans continue the bitter commentary on German social conditions in their essays of the early 1830s. As it had been for earlier critics, Goethe's *Lehrjahre* is the focal point of their attempts to understand and redefine the German novel. Theodor Mundt designates the *Lehrjahre* as the German "*Normal-Roman*," and the "normal" subject matter of the novel the depiction of a journey through the world for the sake of *Bildung* (1833, 95-96). Although the Young German writers regret the stress on the private individual in Goethe's novel, they place the blame on the unfortunate state of eighteenth-century German political reality. Ferdinand Gustav Kühne, for example, attributes Wilhelm Meister's immaturity at the end of the novel to the nonexistence of the German state in Goethe's time: "Um aber Mann zu werden, dazu gehört ein Staat, den Staat kannte aber Goethe gar nicht" [But to become a man you need a state, but Goethe knew no state] (1835, 119). With the exception of Ludwig Börne, the Young Germans do not reject Goethe directly; but they consign his work to the historical past. "Um alles

Slane, Die leiden de jugen Davids.
Davil Meister. Georg Apprentisschf

20   *The German Bildungsroman*

in der Welt keinen Wilhelm wieder," writes Ludolf Wienbarg, "Der ist
abgethan, der ist Göthe's und seiner Zeit" [Never again Wilhelm at any price
... he is passé, he belongs to Goethe and his time] (1835, 115; see Steinecke
1984, 105).

The relegation of Goethe and his work to the past went hand in hand with
attempts to redefine the role of literature in the present. The Young Germans
sought an inspiring form of contemporary art to counteract what they felt was
Goethe's crippling influence. Heinrich Laube brands existing German novels
a distraction from necessary political changes, and he claims that there will
be no revolution in Germany until such novels are banned (1833, 91). Contemporary authors, he says, have followed Goethe's example in that they
merely copy existing reality. Laube admires the artistic talent that enabled
Goethe to illuminate contemporary conditions but laments his failure to direct
future reform (93). Now is the time for novels that *invent* reality, Laube
continues, for works that inspire change. The results of this appeal were not
altogether favorable, however. This literary program encouraged the production of *Tendenzromane* [tendentious novels] that preached virtue rather than
works that developed a critical portrait of existing reality. Moreover, the
novels of the Young Germans did not reach the broad-based public their
democratic agenda sought to attract. As we read in a secret report to
Metternich on the subversive writers, the Young Germans had in fact never
attempted to appeal to the masses. They found their support among the educated members of society (Steinecke 1975, 116).

Ironically, the novel that came closest to fulfilling the aesthetic program
of the Young Germans was written by a man who maintained a critical distance from the radical movement. Karl Leberecht Immermann's *Die Epigonen*
[The Epigons, i.e., "Those Born After"] (1836) depicts the life of a young
man in Germany after the Napoleonic era. Immermann's concentration on the
development of a single protagonist reflects the influence of Goethe's
Lehrjahre, but at the same time he offers a panoramic view of German society during the Restoration. Immermann uses the novel to address such contemporary issues as political radicalism, the fate of the aristocracy, and the
rise of industrialism. In an enthusiastic review, Heinrich Laube praises
Immermann for having updated the Goethean Bildungsroman into the portrait
of an entire age (1836; on the Young German reception of *Die Epigonen* see
Steinecke 1975, 101-04).

Unfortunately for the Young Germans, Immermann's novel appeared after
their publications were officially banned in 1835 and therefore had little
immediate effect on literary production. By the 1840s the dominant influence
of the historical novel on German literature had yielded to that of the French
and English social novel. The German writers again seemed behind the times,
and they again explained their inability to contribute significantly to this

European development by invoking the peculiarities of German history. German literature will not develop freely until the state is reformed, argues Adolf Stahr. In his view, the young Goethe had already realized that the deficiencies in Germany's political life hindered the development of its literature (1842, 164). More optimistic critics sought to effect change through literature that extended the possibility of *Bildung* to a broader segment of society. "Es soll nicht ewig eine Aristokratie der Bildung geben" [There should not always be an aristocracy of *Bildung*], writes Berthold Auerbach (1843, 171).

Robert Prutz's essay "Über die Unterhaltungsliteratur, insbesondere der Deutschen" [On Popular Literature, Particularly That of the Germans] (1845) offers a good example of an attempt to pull German literature back into the European mainstream by reaching out to a broader public. Prutz situates his argument in a philosophy of history that sees the current impoverished age as the inevitable first stage in a process that will lead to a higher level of German culture and — implicitly — to greater political freedom. While conservative critics extolled the virtues of a few canonical writers, Prutz decided to take seriously the sort of popular literature most people actually read. In his view, it is only natural that the overworked, politically disenfranchised masses turn to popular literature for distraction. More heretically still, Prutz claims that the German classics are boring: "was gut ist in der deutschen Literatur, das ist langweilig, und das Kurzweilige ist schlecht" [what is good in German literature is boring, and what is entertaining is bad] (215). Earlier critics had defended the Bildungsroman *despite* its belonging to the popular genre of the novel; Prutz takes German literature to task *because* its best products fail to have mass appeal.

In light of the sorry state of affairs in Germany, Prutz praises French and English social novelists for their ability to be both good and entertaining. Prutz concludes his essay by proposing Berthold Auerbach's *Dorfgeschichten* [village tales] as the solution to the dilemma facing German writers. This new genre promised to provide a healthy German social realism based on the strength of the peasantry rather than the decadent city dwellers of French and English urban realism. Like the Young Germans before him, Prutz encountered both practical problems and theoretical contradictions in his attempts to enlist the masses in a literary revolution. The realism of the *Dorfgeschichte* was by definition partial at best, as it excluded any depiction of the rapidly expanding German cities. Although Prutz begins by defending what people actually read, he gradually drifts toward prescribing what they *ought* to be reading. In the end Prutz's efforts were not rewarded: members of the lower classes who read at all continued to read popular fiction and not the *Dorfgeschichte*. Meanwhile, the Bildungsroman remained in the hands of a politically conservative cultural elite that was to assume power soon after Germany's first attempt to establish a democratic government failed (on Prutz, see Steinecke 1975, 180-200, and Hohendahl 1988, 1989).

2: Ideology and the German Bildungsroman (1848-1945)

The failure of the 1848 revolution dealt a severe blow to German liberalism and brought an end to the politically engaged literary criticism of the *Vormärz* [the period of social unrest that culminated in the uprisings of March, 1848]. Critics who had once reached out to a broad public in newspapers and magazines retreated into an academic discourse accessible only to themselves. This turn away from political activism brought about a renewed interest in the virtues of personal cultivation: "The emphatic notion of education (*Bildung*) strategically supplants in literary theory the notion of political tendency, from which the writers of this period wish to free (poetic) writing" (Hohendahl 1988, 259).

The rise of academic literary criticism after 1848 awakened new interest in Hegel's *Vorlesungen über die Ästhetik* [Lectures on Aesthetics]. Hegel had delivered his lectures in Berlin in 1823, 1826, and 1828-29. Heinrich Gustav Hotho edited the lecture notes, and published them in three volumes between 1835 and 1838. They constitute the major exception to the general decline of formal aesthetics during the *Vormärz*; as they became influential for the discussion of the Bildungsroman primarily in the later nineteenth century, I have postponed their discussion until now.

That Hegel devotes only a few pages to the novel in three volumes on art reveals the influence of a classical aesthetics that had no place for the modern genre. Some have argued that Hegel's major contribution to the novel was actually his own philosophy, and have read the *Phänomenologie des Geistes* [Phenomenology of the Spirit] (1807) as a philosophical Bildungsroman. The brief comments on the genre in the lectures on aesthetics are, nevertheless, extremely suggestive. Hegel argues that the novel is a modern middle-class epic written at a time when the totality of the ancient world has been lost. Reality has become prosaic, and poetry is preserved only in the individual hero. Thus, the novel portrays the conflict between the "Poesie des Herzens" [poetry of the heart] and the "Prosa der Verhältnisse" [prose of the surroundings]. Although Hegel does not mention Goethe explicitly in this context, his reference to the typical subject matter of the modern novel as the apprenticeship or education of the individual against the demands of existing reality clearly reveals which work he adopts as his model for the genre (216). He goes on to offer a sarcastic commentary on the inevitable outcome of this conflict:

Denn das Ende solcher Lehrjahre besteht darin, daß sich das Subjekt
die Hörner abläuft, mit seinem Wünschen und Meinen sich in die
bestehenden Verhältnisse und die Vernünftigkeit derselben hineinbil-
det, in die Verkettung der Welt eintritt, und in ihr sich einen angemes-
senen Standpunkt erwirbt. Mag einer auch noch so viel sich mit der
Welt herumgezankt haben, umhergeschoben worden seyn, zuletzt
bekömmt er meistens doch sein Mädchen und irgend eine Stellung,
heirathet, und wird ein Philister so gut wie die Anderen auch; die
Frau steht der Haushaltung vor, Kinder bleiben nicht aus, das angebe-
tete Weib, das erst die Einzige, ein Engel war, nimmt sich ohngefähr
ebenso aus wie alle Anderen, das Amt giebt Arbeit und Verdrüßlich-
keiten, die Ehe Hauskreuz, und so ist der ganze Katzenjammer der
Uebrigen da. (216-17)

[For such years of apprenticeship end when the subject sows his wild
oats, schools his desires and opinions to conform to current circumstances and to accept their rationality, and takes up a suitable position
in the social network. No matter how much he once quarreled with the
world or was shoved around, in the end he usually gets his girl and
some sort of job, marries, and becomes a Philistine like everybody
else. The wife runs the household, children arrive, and the adored
wife, who was once the only one, an angel, looks more or less like
everyone else. The job provides work and annoyances, the marriage
vexation, and so he has the same hangover as everyone else.]

By focusing on the inevitably problematic conclusion to the Bildungsroman
Hegel places his finger on a sore point that will preoccupy generations of later
critics. The precise target of his sarcasm has been a matter of some debate.
He may be ridiculing Goethe's decision to impose a happy ending on his
novel or, more broadly, pointing out that the reconciliation between individual
and reality can only be achieved in the modern world with resignation. It has
been objected that Hegel does not refer to the average individual but to the
exalted romantic dreamer, the "überspannte Seele" whose unrealistic expectations inevitably lead to disappointment. Rolf Selbmann (1984, 17) offers a
particularly intriguing viewpoint in suggesting that Hegel does not so much
ridicule the *Lehrjahre* as he does the popular "novels of education" prevalent
around 1800. I would add that Hegel's sarcasm serves equally well to counter
the uncritically affirmative readings of Goethe's text of the sort first produced
by Körner (on the *Phenomenology* as a Bildungsroman see Abrams 1971,
225-37 and Jacobs 1972, 100-05; on necessary resignation see Jacobs 1972,
19 and Steinecke 1984, 98; on the romantic dreamer see Hans Jürgen

Schings's comment in Steinecke 1984, 115; also Jacobs 1989, 24-25; on the "novel of education" see Germer 1982).

Friedrich Theodor Vischer expands on Hegel's remarks in his own theory of the novel in his *Aesthetik* (1857). Vischer, too, considers the novel the modern form of the epic. The task of the novelist is to rescue scraps of poetry — what Vischer terms "grüne Stellen" [green spaces] — from an increasingly prosaic world (259-60). The best way to do this, he argues, is to turn away from the public sphere and concentrate on the private realm of the family, individuality, and interiority. The theme of the novel lies in the conflict between this inner life and the rigor of the outer world (261). In addition to Hegel's dominant influence, we hear echoes of Blanckenburg's stress on the hero's inner development; and Vischer cites Schiller's commentary on the *Lehrjahre* in his summarizing statement on the goal of the typical protagonist:

> Das Ziel des Romanhelden ist schließlich immer die Humanität, irgendwie gilt von jedem, was Schiller vom Wilh. Meister sagt: er [Wilhelm] trete von einem leeren und unbestimmten Ideal in ein bestimmtes, thätiges Leben, aber ohne die idealisirende Kraft dabei einzubüßen. (262)

> [The goal of the novel-hero is ultimately always humanity. What Schiller says of Wilhelm Meister is in some sense true for all: he {Wilhelm} steps from an empty and unspecified ideal into a specific active life, but without losing the idealizing energy in the process.]

Thus, Vischer stands squarely in a tradition that stretches back through Hegel and Schiller to the first German theory of the novel.

This tradition was not unbroken, however, for Vischer writes in the wake of several decades of attempts to enlist the novel in the political struggle. Vischer's *Ästhetik* takes part in the general reaction against this trend. For example, Arthur Schopenhauer writes that the quality of a novel depends on the extent to which the author excludes external reality and concentrates on the inner life (1851-60, 233). Vischer also insists that the novel should not focus on great events of historical significance but on that which is purely human, "das Allgemeine des menschlichen Lebens" [that which is common to human life] (262). Although Vischer acknowledges that the novel has become a legitimate genre, he adopts a critical attitude toward dominant trends in actual literary production: the historical and the social novel. He argues that the historical novel contains an internal contradiction, as it tries to depict both the political fate of an entire people and the private life of the hero. As a result, the reader is torn between pondering the fate of nations and wondering if Hans will get his Gretel (266).

Vischer reserves this sort of criticism for the historical novel. When he turns to the role of love and the family in what he terms the "normal species" of the novel, namely "der *bürgerliche* Roman" (266), the sarcasm that marked Hegel's comments on the hero as Philistine is noticeably absent. He asserts piously that the family hearth is the true center of the world in the novel (266). This new, positive stress on the family as a buffer against an increasingly technological world is typical of the later nineteenth century. Not coincidentally, the first issue of *Die Gartenlaube* [The Garden Bower] had appeared just four years before the publication of Vischer's *Aesthetik*. This was a new type of journal that adopted the explicit apoliticism of Schiller's classical aesthetics in its initial statement of purpose but targeted the family, rather than the intellectual community as its audience. The title page of the first issue includes an illustration of a family gathered around a grandfatherly figure who reads aloud within the protective embrace of summer foliage.

Adalbert Stifter evidences the same reverence for family in *Der Nachsommer* [Indian Summer] (1857). Heinrich Drendorf, the hero of this Austrian Bildungsroman, experiences a sheltered youth among loving parents. On one of his solitary wanderings he is taken in by the Freiherr von Risach, a nobleman who has retired to his estate. Eventually Heinrich falls in love with Natalie, the daughter of a woman named Mathilde who lives nearby. As it turns out, Mathilde and Risach had once been in love, but they have overcome their passion and now live as friendly neighbors. Stifter embeds this tale of painful renunciation in a long narrative otherwise without conflict that culminates in Heinrich and Natalie's happy marriage. At their wedding Risach advises Heinrich that his first duty is to establish a pure and noble family order. "Die Familie ist es, die unsern Zeiten not tut" [The family is what our times need], he insists, much more than art, science, progress, or all those other things that seem so desirable (715).

While Stifter's *Nachsommer* culminates in a celebration of the nuclear family, Gottfried Keller's *Der grüne Heinrich* [Green Henry] stands as its negative counterpart. The Swiss author published the first version of his autobiographical novel in 1854-55. Its protagonist, Heinrich Lee, receives his nickname from the color of his clothing, which his mother sews from the remnants of his deceased father's wardrobe. Heinrich grows up in a fatherless family and never manages to establish his own. After being expelled from school he decides to become a landscape painter, only to discover years later that he has no real talent. He returns from a lengthy stay in Germany to learn that his mother has died in poverty during his absence. His self-esteem shattered, Heinrich withdraws into himself and dies. Keller summed up what he termed "the moral of my book": "derjenige, dem es nicht gelingt, die

Verhältnisse seiner Person und seiner Familie in sicherer Ordnung zu erhalten, [ist] auch unbefähigt, im bürgerlichen Leben seine wirksame Stellung einzunehmen" [He who fails to maintain himself and his family in secure order is also unfit to assume an active role in bourgeois society] (in Ermatinger 1915-16, 264). In a substantially revised version of the novel (1879-80) Heinrich survives to become a melancholy bureaucrat, but he remains unmarried.

With the new emphasis on family values in the novel comes a reassertion of the masculinity of the Bildungsroman. For Vischer, the typical novel of the genre tells the story of the youth who struggles through experiences until he finally becomes a man. Love plays an important role in this process, as encounters with female characters serve to further male development:

> In dieser Erziehung ist denn die Liebe, da wir das rein Menschliche, Ideale im Weibe symbolisch anschauen, ein wesentliches Moment und zugleich Surrogat für die verlorene Poesie der heroisch-epischen Weltanschauung. (262)

> [Love is an essential factor in this education, for we view that which is purely human, ideals, symbolically in the woman. At the same time this love is a surrogate for the lost poetry of the heroic-epic world-view.]

In this passage Vischer links his view of the female character to the historico-philosophical premises that underlie his theory of the novel: the woman functions as a poetic oasis in the desert of modernity.

Not all critics of the 1850s adopted Vischer's reverent attitude toward Germany's classical age. Julian Schmidt is particularly critical, accusing the Germans of having lost touch with their roots to produce castles in the air in works that represent a flight from reality (1855, 428). Schmidt takes particular umbrage at Wilhelm Meister's willingness to sacrifice his own desires to the demands of society and challenges the wisdom of Goethean resignation as a response to current needs. Would it not be better to strive boldly to attain one's desires? (in Peschken 1972, 85). This sort of comment allows Bernd Peschken to champion Schmidt's view as a progressive alternative to Wilhelm Dilthey's conservatism. At the same time, however, Peschken ignores less attractive aspects of Schmidt's critique of *Wilhelm Meister*, such as his petit-bourgeois disapproval of Meister's aimless and unprofitable wanderings and his moralizing rejection of the unbridled sensualism of Goethe's novel: "Einen Schritt weiter, und wir wären im Schmutz" [One step further and we would be in filth] (in Mandelkow 1980, 148).

The political union of Germany in 1871 brought an end to public criticism of the classical heritage. In the *Kaiserreich* the Olympian Goethe and *Machtpolitiker* Bismarck were hailed as the twin pillars of Germany's spiritual and military greatness. By this time the German literary canon had become firmly established by literary historians who sought to create a national cultural identity that was to prepare the way for political unification. Once that goal had been attained, the freshly minted canon served to legitimate existing authority. The new government put German literature into service for the state and institutionalized its study. Hence, the last decades of the nineteenth century witness the establishment of *Germanistik* as a separate discipline at the universities, the growth of academic publications aimed at a specialized audience, and the substitution of German literature for the classics as the basis for education in the primary and secondary schools (on Bismarck and Goethe see Mandelkow 1980, 208-9; on the building of a national literature and the institutionalization of its study see Hohendahl 1989, 143, 201-47; on the resulting legitimation of authority see Peschken 1972).

What has traditionally been considered the *locus classicus* of the definition of the Bildungsroman occurs in Wilhelm Dilthey's biography of Friedrich Schleiermacher, where Dilthey proposes the term *Bildungsroman* for German novels written under the direct influence of *Wilhelm Meisters Lehrjahre* (1870, 317). For several reasons, this passage no longer seems as epoch-making as it once did. Both Morgenstern and Vischer had used the term already, although Dilthey evidently believes he is introducing it. More important, nineteenth-century critics had long since identified these works as central to the history of the German novel. When Dilthey points out the immeasurable influence of Goethe's text on subsequent novelists, he is merely repeating a critical commonplace. Moreover, Dilthey's proposed term did not win general acceptance immediately, perhaps because it occurs in the biography of a theologian rather than a work of literary criticism. Yet Dilthey's work does serve as a convenient point of departure for the history of the genre between 1870 and 1945, a period marked by the increasing entanglement of literary history and political ideology. In a significant coincidence, the genre receives its name just as Germany is about to attain political unity.

The logic that governed the process of canon formation in Germany created a critical environment in which the Bildungsroman could flourish. Literary historians from Gervinus to Dilthey structured their work in response to a simple question: "How should earlier authors be related to the Weimar Dioscuri?" (Hohendahl 1989, 151). Goethe and Schiller became the absolute reference point against which to measure the lesser achievements of all previous and subsequent authors. In the process, the literary historians transferred the concept of *Bildung* from the individual human being to the national literature, which records the ripening of the German spirit. Thus, the Bildungsroman becomes the privileged genre of German literature: the organic development of the hero toward maturation and social integration reproduces in miniature the movement of German literature toward its maturity, and this literature, in turn, is to inspire the unification of the German nation.

Dilthey's most influential definition of the genre appeared several decades later in *Das Erlebnis und die Dichtung* [Experience and Poetry] (1906). In an essay on Friedrich Hölderlin, Dilthey reworks passages from his *Leben Schleiermachers* [Schleiermacher's Life] to identify works of Goethe, Jean Paul, Tieck, Novalis, and Hölderlin as examples of the Bildungsroman:

> Von dem Wilhelm Meister und dem Hesperus ab stellen sie alle den Jüngling jener Tage dar; wie er in glücklicher Dämmerung in das Leben eintritt, nach verwandten Seelen sucht, der Freundschaft begegnet und der Liebe, wie er nun aber mit den harten Realitäten der Welt in Kampf gerät und so unter mannigfachen Lebenserfahrungen heranreift, sich selber findet und seiner Aufgabe in der Welt gewiß wird. (393-94)

> [Beginning with Wilhelm Meister and Hesperus, they all depict the youth of that time, how he enters life in a blissful daze, searches for kindred souls, encounters friendship and love, but then how he comes into conflict with the hard realities of the world and thus matures in the course of manifold life-experiences, finds himself, and becomes certain of his task in the world.]

Taken out of context, the passage seems to repeat a conservative understanding of the genre that emphasizes the hero's ultimate triumph and implicitly affirms the surrounding society. It was this aspect of Dilthey's definition that was to prove most important for critics in the first half of the twentieth century and that provoked later charges of ideology (Peschken 1972). On closer examination, however, Dilthey's understanding of the Bildungsroman appears considerably more complex.

Christian Gottfried Körner had argued that the individual and the world attain perfect equilibrium at the end of *Wilhelm Meisters Lehrjahre*. In contrast, Dilthey points out that Goethe creates harmony at the novel's conclusion only by deliberately repressing personal idiosyncracies, grinding experience, and destructive passion: "Der spröde Stoff des Lebens ist ausgeschieden" [The difficult material of life is eliminated] (1906, 329). Dilthey further qualifies his seemingly affirmative assessment of the Bildungsroman by situating the novels in historical context. He identifies the era of the Bildungsroman as an age long past that the current reader can read about with nostalgia. At the same time, he points out that the stress on inner development in these novels compensates for the fact that the *Bürger* around 1800 were excluded from meaningful participation in the public sphere. Taken together, Dilthey's comments yield a deliberately ambivalent picture: while he admires the idealism of the young heroes in these works, he considers extravagant their expenditure of feeling in a struggle against an old world order that they were bound to lose. In short, Dilthey views the Bildungsroman as the product of a bygone era, one touched by the golden light of nostalgia, but one that records the futile struggle of introverted heroes to assert themselves against the power of a bureaucratic, military state.

Dilthey's major contribution to aesthetics, *Die Einbildungskraft des Dichters* [The Poetic Imagination] (1887), confirms the impression that he feels the time for the Bildungsroman has past. In the closing pages of this work Dilthey adopts a messianic tone, claiming that the Germans are living at the dawn of "the third age" (239). The novel has become the dominant form of the modern epic, and Dilthey anticipates the coming of the great German novelist. Yet he does not call for a new Goethe who will continue the tradition of the *Lehrjahre*: times have changed, and the poets of the past cannot move us as they moved their contemporaries. Dilthey looks instead to the novelists of England and France for inspiration: what Germany needs now is a German Dickens, Flaubert, or Zola who will write the great novel of Berlin (240-41).

Dilthey's appeal to France and England for the solution to a crisis in German literature reflects a general trend in the last decades of the nineteenth century. Eberhard Lämmert has argued that the publication of Emile Zola's *Le Roman Experimental* in 1880 marks an important turning point in the history of the German novel (1975, xiii). The widespread discussion of this naturalist work once again thrust the difference between the European social novel and the German Bildungsroman into the foreground. Yet the German discourse about the Bildungsroman that begins to take shape in the first decades of the twentieth century does not rely exclusively on rigid distinctions between the two traditions. The German *Sonderweg* [special path] leads through terrain occupied by the dominant social novel, and the definition of the national literature proceeds through both rejection and assimilation of foreign influence.

Heinrich Driesmans's short article "Der alte und der neue Erziehungs-roman" [The Old and the New *Erziehungsroman*] (1904) marks one phase in this process. Unlike Dilthey, who views the Bildungsroman as a thing of the past, Driesmans extends the history of what he terms the *Erziehungsroman* up through the nineteenth century. He argues that the protagonists of such works as *Agathon*, *Wilhelm Meisters Lehrjahre*, and Jean Paul's *Titan* (1800-03) are psychologically unproblematic individuals representative of their era who strike out boldly into the world, eventually discover their limitations, and resign themselves to useful activity in society. In the course of the nineteenth century Driesmans notes a gradual change, as novelists begin to reveal an interest in what he terms "das genealogische Moment" (249), a sort of Darwinian interest in questions of heredity, race, and breeding. Novelists no longer portray healthy, typical figures but concentrate on the psychopathology of the abnormal individual who is viewed as the product of "eine hereditäre Verelendung und physiologische Verarmung" [a hereditary deterioration and physiological impoverishment] (249). He traces this process through some lesser-known works and authors around the turn of the century and concludes by designating Thomas Mann's *Buddenbrooks* (1901) the typical tragical *Erziehungsroman* of his time (250).

Driesmans's essay is important for two reasons: he sees the development of the nineteenth-century German novel as the continuation of a tradition begun in the eighteenth century, not as a new departure; and he sees the German novel moving in the direction of the European naturalist novel. As the German Bildungsroman becomes increasingly interested in psychopathology it comes closer to the European novel of Naturalism; or, in other words, the naturalist novel is a sick Bildungsroman! Seemingly dissatisfied with this degenerating teleology, Driesmans hopes for a novel that would encourage a sense of reverent responsibility for the needs of the current generation (250).

Two years later Herman Anders Krüger offered a much more positive assessment in "Der neuere deutsche Bildungsroman" [The More Recent German Bildungsroman] (1906). Like Driesmans, Krüger traces the continuous history of the Bildungsroman from the eighteenth century to his own time. Yet his remarks reveal a new, fervent nationalism. Already in Jeremias Gotthelf's *Uli der Knecht* [Uli the Farm-Hand] (1841) — the story of a Swiss peasant who makes good — Krüger identifies a "genuinely German [*sic!*] disposition" (258). He goes on to praise Gustav Freytag's "thoroughly national art" and sees in Wilhelm Raabe's novels evidence of the same German virtues (267). While we can trace the tendency to link the German national character with the tradition of the Bildungsroman at least to the Brockhaus article of 1817, Krüger gives the argument a new twist: now it is not merely the novel that reflects a particular German trait, but Germany as a whole that is viewed as the hero of its own Bildungsroman! Krüger identifies the year of German unification as an important stage in the development of the national character: German military prowess provides external confirmation of the spiritual maturation of the German people (267).

Having charted the emergence of the nation to this provisional high point, Krüger is forced to acknowledge that the naturalist and symbolist movements of the late nineteenth century retarded the development of the German Bildungsroman. Yet he decries those who lament the absence of a genuinely German contribution to the novel:

> Seit Goethe besitzen wir ... eine Romanart, die ein ganz ausgesprochen nationales Gepräge trägt ... den deutschen Bildungsroman, der im letzten Jahrhundert ganz eigentlich der Roman der Dichter und Denker war und es voraussichtlich auch bleiben wird. (270)

> [Since Goethe we have possessed ... a type of novel with very pronounced national features ... the German Bildungsroman, which was truly the novel of poets and thinkers in the past century, and which it presumably will remain.]

Krüger shares his pride in the German novel with his contemporary Karl Rehorn, who in the same year proposed healthy German novels in the tradition of the *Lehrjahre* as the antidote to the corrupting influence of decadent French Naturalism. Krüger himself, however, does not view the Bildungsroman in direct opposition to the naturalist novel. Rather, he envisions a fusion of German inwardness with the acknowledged advances of Naturalism (271). Exactly what this synthesis will look like does not emerge clearly in Krüger's essay; he mentions the novels of a certain Wilhelm von Polenz with marked reservations and yet concludes by stressing his confidence that the peculiarly German form of the novel will prove resilient enough to absorb foreign influence without losing its national identity.

Krüger's national pride recurs in subtler form in Max Wundt's monumental study of Goethe's Wilhelm Meister novels (1913). To be sure, Wundt insists that only the ancient Greeks and the modern Germans have the capacity for genius (81), and he praises Goethe as the defender of the German spirit because he resisted the French Revolution, which had seduced many of his contemporaries to adopt foreign ideas (308). Wundt's cultural conservatism emerges most clearly, however, in the structure of his work as a whole. His monograph appeared just three years after the rediscovery of Goethe's first version of the novel, and Wundt gives equal weight to all three stages of the project. In his view, only the *Lehrjahre* is a Bildungsroman; the *Sendung* portrays a genius seeking to found a German national theater, while the *Wanderjahre*, which Wundt dubs a *Kulturroman*, moves the focus away from the individual to society as a whole. Between these works lies the *Lehrjahre*, whose aim is to portray the harmonious development [*Ausbildung*] of an entire personality (194).

Wundt's view of the *Lehrjahre* itself is not particularly original, although he does qualify his optimistic reading of the text by stressing that the goal of *Bildung* is limited for each individual; only humanity as a whole attains "das

Ideal einer harmonischen Ausbildung" (280). More provocative is the broader perspective within which he situates his study. At first glance Wundt's effort appears to be nothing more than an exhaustive close reading of the three novels. But in fact he seeks to portray the spirit of the age in which Goethe lived. Here Goethe's special status comes to his aid. Wundt views Goethe as the epitome of German culture; to study his work is to study the awakening of modernity to self-consciousness (5). As Goethe portrays the historical development of the age most directly in his Wilhelm Meister novels, they are best suited to reveal its essential characteristics. Wundt contends further that the Bildungsroman is the "highest form of the novel" (55) and that the *Lehrjahre* is the most significant Bildungsroman, a work vastly superior to the productions of such minor figures as Tieck, Novalis, and Hölderlin (67). In short, contemplation of Goethe provides a short cut to the study of modernity in general and of German culture in particular, and this culture appears in its most condensed form in his contribution to the Bildungsroman.

Emil Ermatinger defends Gottfried Keller's *Der grüne Heinrich* as the true successor to the *Lehrjahre* in his biography of the Swiss writer (1915-16). He shares Wundts's antipathy to what he terms the "egoistic personality cult" of the eighteenth century and the romantics (278), while praising Keller for bringing the novel back into contact with reality. In Ermatinger's view, Keller even surpasses Goethe in this regard. Goethe is primarily interested in the development of the individual. Wilhelm Meister does eventually join a group of philanthropic aristocrats, but their concern for society is that of an enlightened eighteenth-century despotism (273-74). Only Keller provides a paradigmatic example of the modern individual who develops as a social being (278). To be sure, Heinrich Lee falls short of his goal in the first version of the novel, but he succeeds in the second and becomes an effective civil servant. Ermatinger cautions that we should not mistake his development from artist to bureaucrat as a descent into the dreary rhythm of the working world. The drab exterior conceals the glowing light of a life devoted to the common good of humanity (521). Keller's primary achievement in *Der grüne Heinrich* is to extend the literary tradition of the Bildungsroman in a way that evidences increased concern for civic duty.

Like critics before him, Georg Lukács, in his *Theory of the Novel* (1920), grants *Wilhelm Meisters Lehrjahre* representative status. Lukács develops his theory as an extensive commentary on the brief remarks in Hegel's *Vorlesungen über die Ästhetik*, but he also incorporates theories of romantic irony and introduces Kierkegaard's pessimism into Hegel's philosophy of history (18). Composed during the first year of World War I, the book was written in what Lukács described as "a mood of permanent despair over the state of the world" (1962, 12).

Lukács's argument reflects the tradition of German Idealism insofar as it contrasts modernity with antiquity and the novel with the epic. He views the epic as the natural expression of a homogeneous world. The ancient Greeks "knew only answers, but no questions" (31); theirs was a world were the "rift between 'inside' and 'outside' ... the self and the world" did not yet exist (29). We moderns, in contrast, live in an era of "transcendental homelessness," and the novel best expresses our predicament (41). The epic needs no form, because it is already part of a totality; the novel, in contrast, must create totality, "for the natural unity of the metaphysical spheres has been destroyed forever" (37). The epic expresses the values of a unified community; its "hero is, strictly speaking, never an individual" (66), whereas the novel portrays the isolated protagonist in opposition to society.

After mapping out the "transcendental topography" (31) of antiquity and modernity, Lukács constructs a typology of the novel form. He organizes the typology dialectically: the novel of abstract idealism depicts an inwardly unproblematic hero obsessed with an ideal that he seeks to impose on prosaic reality (as in Cervantes's *Don Quixote* 1605-15). The "romanticism of disillusionment" portrays the opposite extreme of a passive, introspective hero who retreats from a hostile environment (for example, Flaubert's *L'Education sentimentale* 1870). Finally, *Wilhelm Meisters Lehrjahre* offers an attempted synthesis, which reconciles the problematic hero with concrete social reality. Goethe envisions an "ideal of free humanity" in a communal context, where the "heroism of abstract idealism and the pure interiority of Romanticism" are "surmounted and integrated in the interiorised order" of a mature individual (133-34).

Lukács's philosophical method invites criticism on a number of levels. As Lukács himself admits in his preface of 1962, the analysis "remains extremely abstract ... cut off from concrete socio-historical realities" 16-17). Lukács reduces the history of the novel to three prototypical texts and relegates all other novels to imperfectly realized variants on his neat dialectic. Moreover, Lukács's idealization of the Greeks falsifies the past and reveals a disturbing nostalgia for "an organicist ideology" that "tends to go hand in hand with retrograde political yearnings" of the sort that "later led to Nazism" (Miles 1979, 29).

In Lukács's defense, we should point out that he does not celebrate *Wilhelm Meisters Lehrjahre* as the triumph of German spirituality, nor does he engage in the sort of patriotic excesses that characterized the beginning of World War I. In fact, he claims in the preface that "the prospect of final victory by the Germany of that time was to me nightmarish" (11). Moreover, Lukács's interpretation of Goethe's novel displays a subtlety often lacking in descriptions of the Bildungsroman. In his estimation, Goethe's novel offers only an *attempted* synthesis between the individual and society, one that necessarily falls short of its goal. Although the novel seeks to portray the possibility of free humanity for all, Goethe recognizes that the ideal must be restricted in practice to the members of the nobility. Lukács also notes the discomfort evident in Goethe's use of the "fantastic apparatus" of "the mysterious tower, the all-knowing initiates with their providential actions, etc." (142). Goethe strains to grant universal validity to a purely individual experience but in the end cannot disguise the fact that he does not inhabit "a stable and secure transcendent world" (137); the fissures of modernity cannot be disguised, "no artist's skill is great and masterly enough to bridge the abyss" (143).

Writing on Thomas Mann's reception of Nietzsche, Stanley Corngold says that Mann's seeming reversals of opinion regarding the philosopher can be reduced to a common denominator: "Mann never reads Nietzsche except to discover in him a rhetoric for affirming attractively his own position" (1986, 156). The same could be said of Mann's comments on the Bildungs- or *Entwicklungsroman* (he uses the two terms interchangeably). Mann wrote his first extensive comments on the genre in a newspaper article published in 1916, at the height of his enthusiasm for Germany's involvement in World War I. Here Mann sounds the familiar theme that the socially critical novel is not a particularly German genre. There is, however, he continues, one sort of novel that is "typically German, legitimately-national": the Bildungsroman. Echoing Dilthey, Mann links the genre to the *Humanitätsbegriff* [concept of humanity] that emerged in the late eighteenth century as compensation for the private individual's exclusion from political power. The Bildungsroman is thus in Mann's eyes intimately connected with the German romantic tradition of apolitical individualism. He views the development of the German novel in the later nineteenth century as a process of moving away from this national genre toward the adoption of some highly un-German tendencies: politicization, literarization, intellectualization, radicalization — in short, "die Demokratisierung Deutschlands" — which causes the decline of the Bildungsroman. Although Mann laments the passing of the conservative climate that nourished the Bildungsroman, he acknowledges that historical developments are irreversible. He argues somewhat paradoxically that if the increase in critical intellect caused the genre's deterioration, it is only by tapping into this destructive force that the genre can be revitalized. Mann therefore concludes that the modern Bildungsroman can only be written as a parody of a past tradition, as the autobiography of a confidence man (117), i.e., as his own *Bekenntnisse des Hochstaplers Felix Krull* [Confessions of the Confidence-Man Felix Krull] (begun in 1911, published in 1954).

Mann expands on the themes sounded in this short article in his *Betrachtungen eines Unpolitischen* [Reflections of an Unpolitical Man] (1918). Once again he asserts a causal connection between democratization and the rise of the social novel, on the one hand, and the corresponding eclipse of the authentically German tradition of the Bildungsroman, on the other (68-70). He also once again introduces *Felix Krull* as the necessary parody of the genre in an unpropitious era (101). Placing his current opposition to French "civilization" in the long tradition of German hostility to France, and aligning himself in particular with Goethe's rejection of the French Revolution, Mann insists on the essential bond between the German concept of *Bildung* and the German aversion to politics:

> Denn auch darüber kann kein Zweifel sein, daß Bildung, 'ruhige' Bildung, wie Goethe sie dem Franztum, das heißt: der Politik entgegenstellt, *quietistisch* stimmt und daß das tief unpolitische, antiradikale und antirevolutionäre Wesen der Deutschen zusammenhängt mit der bei ihnen errichteten Oberherrschaft der Bildungsidee. (506)

> [For there can also be no doubt that *Bildung*, the "quiet" *Bildung* Goethe opposes to *Franztum* (French-ness), i.e. politics, inclines toward *quietism*, and that the deeply apolitical, antiradical, and antirevolutionary character of the Germans is linked to the concept of *Bildung*, which they have raised to a position of supreme authority among them.]

Within a few years, however, Thomas Mann has reversed his understanding of the Bildungsroman. In his essay on Goethe and Tolstoy he recalls the stress on subjective personal development represented in the *Lehrjahre* (1922, 67). Yet he now goes on to include the *Wanderjahre* in his discussion, where he sees a turn toward objective, social concerns (68). The "unpolitical man" who just a few years earlier had railed against the corruption of a truly German genre of personal cultivation now hails Goethe as the author of an increasingly public, democratic, even political novel (150). Thus, in a talk delivered in June 1923 Mann can cite the Wilhelm Meister novels as a remarkable anticipation of the German progress from inwardness to objectivity, politics, and democracy (855). Mann had already proclaimed his allegiance to the new Weimar Republic in his pivotal essay "Von deutscher Republik" [On the German Republic] (1922a). Near its conclusion he argues that the Romantic fascination with disease and death is actually an expression of interest in life and humanity. He goes on to propose that this insight could form the basis of a Bildungsroman; it would demonstrate that in the final analysis, death is an experience of life (11: 851).

The project was already well under way, and in 1924 Mann published the result in two thick volumes as *Der Zauberberg* (The Magic Mountain). Here Mann unfolds the tale of a young engineer from Hamburg, Hans Castorp,

who travels to a sanatorium in Switzerland to visit his ailing cousin. He plans
to stay for only a few weeks but ends up spending seven years before the
outset of World War I finally pulls him off the mountain. The most significant passage in the novel occurs several hundred pages earlier in the chapter
"Schnee" [Snow]. Lost in a blizzard at high altitude, the exhausted Castorp
has an allegorical dream of a beautiful Mediterranean people who maintain
their charm and decorum despite their awareness of destructive Dionysian
passions. Mann italicizes the sentence that sums up the dream's significance:
*"Der Mensch soll um der Güte und Liebe willen dem Tode keine Herrschaft
einräumen über seine Gedanken"* [*For the sake of goodness and love man
should not grant death any power over his thoughts*] (686). He thereby adapts
the German Bildungsroman to give poetic expression to his new political ideas
(on Mann's evolving understanding of the Bildungsroman see Scharfschwerdt
1967, esp. 110-13, 165-66).

   In 1933 Hermann Weigand published a book-length study of *Der
Zauberberg* that situates the work in literary tradition without losing sight of
the particular historical situation in which it was written. Weigand argues that
Mann's work is at once an example of the pedagogical, the philosophic, and
the symbolic novel, but he contends that it is above all an example of the
Bildungsroman, "that aristocratic and exclusive group among the novels of
self-development which constitutes Germany's most distinctive contribution
to the world's fiction" (4). Mann's novel portrays "the transformation of this
simple young man [Hans Castorp] into a genius in the realm of experience"
(5). But *Der Zauberberg* offers far more than the account of one individual's
growth. In Weigand's view, Castorp's preference for philosophical contemplation over action, his love for music, and his distrust of language all contribute to his role as a symbolic German. In the course of the novel Castorp
gradually overcomes his "native indifference to language" (117) under the
Italian Settembrini's eloquent influence. Herein lies "Thomas Mann's postwar message to Germany," a country that is

> most seriously in need of modifying her native aversion to logical
> clarity and psychological analysis. For the sake of living up to her
> reputed universality, she needs to incline herself consciously to the
> rational pole without fear of endangering her irrational substratum.
> (125)

Taken as a whole, the novel stands as "a summons and an imperative" to its
readers (126), pointing "the way to a new faith in life, to a quickened consciousness of things really mattering" (vii). Yet Weigand also concedes that
Mann's attempt to redirect Germany away from its irrational tendencies has
put *Der Zauberberg* "upon the index by the conservative wing of the German

intellectuals" (125). The date of Weigand's preface — January 1933 — stands as an ironic commentary on the failed hopes offered by Mann's novel, as historical events were soon to overtake Mann's well-intentioned plea for greater humanism in a Germany rapidly descending into barbarism.

Several important studies of the Bildungsroman written for an academic audience during the 1920s and 1930s avoided direct engagement in political issues. In this context Christine Touaillon's article on the Bildungsroman in the *Reallexikon der deutschen Literaturgeschichte* (1925-26) deserves mention for a number of reasons. Its very existence indicates that by the 1920s the Bildungsroman had become enough of a fixed generic concept to rate inclusion in a dictionary of poetic terms. Touaillon also attempts to distinguish between the *Erziehungsroman*, *Entwicklungsroman*, and Bildungsroman and thereby opens a terminological debate that has continued ever since. Two points are of particular interest: first, Touaillon argues that the Bildungsroman, with its complex mixture of realistic detail and idealistic abstraction, cannot be a popular genre. The claim is hardly new, but it comes at a time when conservative critics sought to hail the genre as the expression of a genuine national popularism. Second, Touaillon, the author of a monumental study of German women writers in the eighteenth century, makes a point of including works by Sophie von LaRoche, Sophie Mereau, and Caroline von Wolzogen in her brief history of the genre. Although this inclusion of texts by women in the canon is not without precedent — Krüger had mentioned works by Marie von Ebner-Eschenbach and Luise von François in his article on the genre — it was certainly unusual, and it went ignored until the renewed interest in women writers in the 1980s.

That Melitta Gerhard's 1926 study *Der deutsche Entwicklungsroman bis zu Goethes "Wilhelm Meister"* was republished without revision in 1968 indicates the extent of its lasting appeal. Particularly influential was her careful distinction of the pedagogical *Erziehungsroman*, in which a mentor instructs a pupil in a fixed educational program, from the *Entwicklungsroman*, a general term applicable to any work focusing on the protagonist's development, and from the Bildungsroman, which she views as the product of the late eighteenth century. By choosing the more general category of the *Entwicklungsroman* as the subject of her monograph, Gerhard is able to extend the history of the genre much further into the past. Rather than beginning with Wieland's *Agathon*, which by then had become standard practice, she goes all the way back to Wolfram von Eschenbach's *Parzival* (1200-1210) and Hans Jakob Grimmelshausen's *Der abenteuerliche Simplicissimus Teutsch* (1669). While conceding the possibility of a non-German *Entwicklungsroman*, she sets out to trace an independent development in the history of the German novel, which she views as a significant segment of the history of the German *Geist* (2). Here again the genre is linked to the German national spirit, although

Gerhard's work does not display the *Hurrah Patriotismus* of a Krüger or later National Socialist critics.

Gerhard views the development of the German *Entwicklungsroman* as a gradual shift in focus from the external world toward the inner life. Although *Parzival* portrays the development of a central character from childhood to maturity, it lacks the self-reflection that characterizes later texts. Internal development becomes evident only through Parzival's changing reaction to external events. Moreover, Wolfram determines the goal of his hero's development in advance; Parzival progresses to his place in an affirmed social and religious order. In contrast, Grimmelshausen's baroque novel offers a stern condemnation of this world in favor of a transcendent religious order. Here we find the beginnings of a turn toward the inner life of the hero as we occasionally encounter moments of psychological analysis in the predominantly didactic tale. Pietist autobiographers of the eighteenth century further develop Grimmelshausen's nascent interest in individual psychology, and Wieland's *Agathon* likewise reflects this new interest. For the first time we encounter an individual who matures through the gradual accumulation of life experiences. The development culminates in *Wilhelm Meisters Lehrjahre*, which in Gerhard's opinion portrays an uninterrupted path of spiritual unfolding (136). Meister develops his innate potential through encounters with his environment. Gerhard draws on Goethe's own morphological concepts of *Bildung* to explain the process. She cites Körner's analysis positively (142) and describes Meister's progress toward unity, wholeness, and harmony with himself (158).

Gerhard's book vastly expands the historical scope of previous studies while offering increased terminological precision in the use of the term *Bildungsroman*. At the same time, however, the expansion also constricts, for like Lukács, Gerhard bases her theory on only a few examples. *Parzival* thus looms up out of the Middle Ages without precursors and seems to have no direct influence for over four hundred years. Moreover, the reconstruction of German literary history in Gerhard's overview culminates in a predictable celebration of *Wilhelm Meisters Lehrjahre*, and conveniently ignores what follows.

Ernst Ludwig Stahl's 1934 study of *Bildung* and the Bildungsroman shares similar strengths and shortcomings with Gerhard's work. Stahl devotes two thirds of his monograph to tracing the concept of *Bildung* in the eighteenth century as it changed from a religious to a secular *humanitätsphilosophischer* concept. His wide-ranging history of ideas remains useful today, as his survey is concise, lucid, and untainted by fascist ideology. In a lengthy final chapter Stahl relates the philosophical concept of *Bildung* to the emergence of the Bildungsroman. Here again he traces this development historically, demonstrating how the new genre marked the confluence of the adventure novel and the Pietist autobiography. In the process we witness the gradual inward turn of the adventure tale and an increasing concern with external reality in writers born into a Pietist tradition. Stahl singles out the autobiographical novels of Jung-Stilling and Moritz for particular attention. Only Wieland's *Agathon* deserves to be termed a Bildungsroman in his view, as here for the first time we have development that leads toward an ideal of *Bildung*; yet even Wieland's novel cannot really be considered an example of the *humanitätsphilosophische* Bildungsroman. Stahl reserves this appellation for *Wilhelm Meisters Lehrjahre*, the first poetic representation of the new philosophical idea.

The strength of Stahl's work lies in its careful attention to the historical development of the concept of *Bildung*; this focus on the *idea* of *Bildung*, however, results in a certain weakness in the section on the Bildungsroman itself. Stahl's argument reduces works that precede the *Lehrjahre* to imperfect stages on the way to the genre's paradigm. For example, he attributes inconsistency in Wieland's *Agathon* to it being written before the concept of *Bildung* had had time to develop fully (159). Thus the teleological argument takes precedence over the specific texts; the problem with *Agathon* is that it is not yet the *Lehrjahre*. The same teleological thinking prohibits Stahl from perceiving any irony in Goethe's novel. Stahl begins with a ready-made philosophical concept and simply applies it to the text; not surprisingly, he too cites Körner enthusiastically (173). Moreover, Stahl implicitly restricts the literary genre to one novel, as all other works mentioned lead up to Goethe, and nothing follows in his wake.

Mikhail Bakhtin's fragmentary study of the Bildungsroman occupies an unusual position in the genre's history. Written between 1936 and 1938, it was not published in Russian until 1979 and was translated into English only in 1986. Unlike the early Lukács, who had insisted on the essential link between the novel and modernity, Bakhtin sees the history of the novel as beginning in antiquity. He does, however, make an important distinction between early novels and the modern Bildungsroman. Bakhtin argues that "the vast majority of novels (and subcategories of novels) know only the image of the *ready-made* hero" (1936-38, 20). The Bildungsroman, in contrast, presents us with "the image of *man in the process of becoming*" (19). Moreover, novels by Rabelais, Grimmelshausen, and Goethe expand the depiction of personal development to include historical change. For Bakhtin, the evolving hero of the Bildungsroman is the lens through which the current transitional era becomes visible as the threshold to something new:

> He emerges *along with the world* and he reflects the historical emergence of the world itself. He is no longer within an epoch, but on the border between two epochs, at the transition point from one to the

other. This transition is accomplished in him and through him ... It is as though the very *foundations* of the world are changing, and man must change along with them. (23-24)

Bakhtin then sketches Goethe's historical consciousness, but the text breaks off before he gets to *Wilhelm Meisters Lehrjahre*. Bakhtin was a heavy smoker, and apparently the acute paper shortage in Stalinist Russia drove him to sacrifice most of his essay for cigarette papers: "He began smoking pages from the conclusion of the manuscript, so what we have is a small portion of its opening section, primarily about Goethe" (Holquist 1986, xiii).

The persistent identification of the Bildungsroman with Germany reached its nadir during the period of National Socialist rule. As Karl Robert Mandelkow has observed in his history of Goethe's reception, not all critics who remained in Germany between 1933 and 1945 were equally guilty of complicity with the criminal regime (1989, 88-89). Yet the historically close association of the Bildungsroman with something essentially German made it particularly susceptible to abuse. Edgar Kirsch's 1937 study "Hans Grimms 'Volk ohne Raum' [Nation, People, or Race without Room] als Bildungsroman" offers a paradigmatic example of the fascist appropriation of *Bildung*. Written in a rapturous, hortatory style, it offers the crassest contribution to the study of the Bildungsroman I have encountered. Grimm's novel appeared in 1926; set in the African colonies, it advocates imperialist expansion as the solution to Germany's lack of *Lebensraum* at home. Its hero is Cornelius Friebott, whom Kirsch salutes as the prototypical Nordic individual: "Seine Gestalt ist sein Schicksal. Schlank und blond und ruhig schreitet er daher" [His body type is his fate. He strides along, slender and blond and calm] (483). At first uncertain of his role in the world, Friebott progresses toward an understanding of his calling — to affirm Germany over everything. "Seine Idee heißt: alles für Deutschland!" (478). The recognition of racial difference and Germanic superiority is an important part of Friebott's development. Kirsch agrees with the editor of the academic journal *Dichtung und Volkstum* (*Euphorion* until 1933 and again after the war), that Friebott represents the German version of the Führer-type, who demands political privilege for the white race (487). Finally, although Kirsch aligns Grimm with Goethe and Keller to acknowledge his contemporary culture's intellectual debt to the past, he also underscores the fundamental transformation in the concept of *Bildung* from the individual to the state, from a personal to a collective ideal.

Charlotte Kehr's Leipzig dissertation on the twentieth-century German *Entwicklungsroman* (1939) also subscribes wholeheartedly to Nazi ideology. Kehr traces a straightforward progression of the German novel away from a dangerously exaggerated individualism toward an ostensibly genuine "völkisch-nationale Tradition" that places the energy of the individual in the service of the *Volk* (82). Practical activity in the community replaces excessive intellectualism in works that reveal a new reverence for the deep roots that bind the Germanic peoples to their ancestral homelands (83). Not surprisingly, Grimm's *Volk ohne Raum* takes a prominent place in this development, which Kehr celebrates as a guide to the political rebirth of a German nation driven away from "die heimatliche Scholle" [its native soil] by a lack of *Lebensraum* (101).

Hans Heinrich Borcherdt produced a particularly disturbing contribution to the history of the German Bildungsroman in his lengthy article of 1941. In many ways his work merely reformulates what had become commonplaces in the study of the genre during the early twentieth century. He traces the familiar path from *Parzival* through *Simplicissimus* to the *Lehrjahre*, for example, and extols Goethe's text as supreme example of the German Bildungsroman before moving on to give honorable mention to Stifter, Keller, and Raabe. Yet many aspects of his essay reveal the influence of Nazi ideology. The strident nationalism already evident in Krüger's 1906 article returns in full force in Borcherdt's text, which repeatedly stresses the peculiarly German nature of the genre. The German connection itself is not new; Borcherdt supports his thesis, however, with appeals to Nazi racial theories. Citing Erwin Guido Kolbenheyer, he argues that the art of a particular people necessarily corresponds to the biological state of development of that *Volk*. The Bildungsroman becomes the timeless expression of the biological life-force of a particular people (210). In Borcherdt's view, Kolbenheyer's *Paracelsus* trilogy portrays a symbolic German who embodies "das Ringen der deutschen Seele um eine neue arteigene Natur- und Welterkenntnis" [the struggle of the German soul for a new, racially-specific understanding of nature and the world] (212). These appeals to the biological specificity (and superiority) of the German peoples are accompanied by a new stress on the group over the individual as the goal of *Bildung* and the Bildungsroman. Borcherdt shares Kehr's enthusiasm for Grimm's fervently nationalistic *Volk ohne Raum*. In his view, it is not just the individual character but also all of Germany that becomes the hero of the novel (209). Thus, Friebott's early love for a racially compatible partner ("ein artgleiches Du," 219) is only a step toward realizing the common yearning of the German *Volk* to establish a community unified by loyalty to the *Heimat* [the German soil] and the willingness to devote its entire life to the service of the *Vaterland*. Borcherdt goes so far as to enlist Goethe in the Nationalist Socialist cause, citing him as an example of a writer who had advocated personal resignation for the communal good. Personal development becomes merely the first stage of a process that leads to the incorporation of the individual into the communal whole (187). *Bildung* has become a means toward the *Gleichschaltung* [forced homogenization] of the German people in a *Blut und Boden* [blood and soil] ideology.

By the 1930s the exiled Thomas Mann had become one of the most prominent German spokesmen against the growing barbarism of the Nazi regime. His comments on the Bildungsroman during this period continue the turn to democracy already evident in his work of the 1920s, but with an increasingly elegiac strain. During World War I Mann had viewed the nineteenth-century novel as a regrettable turning away from German inwardness to imported democracy; by 1939 he sees Goethe's Wilhelm Meister novels as harbingers of a progressive social realism whose promise went unfulfilled in German fiction — a failure even more disturbing for what it reveals about the German antipathy to democracy (1939, 361). In was in this context that Mann composed *Doktor Faustus* (1947), the fictional biography of the German composer Adrian Leverkühn narrated by Leverkühn's friend Serenus Zeitblom. In this densely symbolic work Mann attempts to diagnose the moral and cultural malaise that made Germany susceptible to fascism. His reclusive hero invents a compositional technique modeled on Arnold Schönberg's twelve-tone method in an attempt to overcome the stagnation of late romantic music. Yet in his desire to break through to a new, rigidly structured aesthetic form infused with the irrational energy of precultural barbarism, Leverkühn unwittingly anticipates fascist attempts to revitalize the state through the total indoctrination and mobilization of the German people. Meanwhile, the classical scholar Zeitblom can do nothing but sadly record the demise of both his friend and Germany. At times his impotence turns to implication in Germany's guilt, as when he expresses mild disapproval of his Führer's handling of "the Jewish problem." In the end Leverkühn falls victim to insanity brought on by syphilis. In his last lucid days he composes *Dr. Fausti Weheklag* [Dr. Faustus's Lament], in which he tries to "take back" the humanist faith of Beethoven's Ninth Symphony. By the same token, we can view Mann's novel as a refutation of the inherent optimism of the classical Bildungsroman. With Germany physically destroyed and intellectually bankrupt, the possibility of a return to the genre of the "land of poets and thinkers" seemed remote indeed.

3: Postwar Critics and the German Bildungsroman

Return to Goethe

Literary criticism during the Third Reich had sought to abolish the autonomy of the aesthetic sphere by enlisting properly *völkisch* art in the service of the fascist state. In an effort to avoid the contamination wrought by the politicization of aesthetics and the aesthetization of politics, German critics of the immediate postwar period concentrated on the intrinsic analysis of acknowledged classics. Humiliated by the atrocities of the recent past, critics flocked to Goethe in an effort to unearth a buried humanist legacy from the rubble of Hitler's Germany (Mandelkow 1989, 135; on fascist literary criticism see Berman 1988, 336-43).

One of the most influential critics of the immediate postwar period was Günther Müller, whose many publications of the 1940s and 1950s typify the "morphological turn" in Goethe reception of the period. Goethe's writings on biological form become for Müller the key to the interpretation of both Goethe's life and his literary texts. This approach informs his 1948 study of *Wilhelm Meisters Lehrjahre:* "Was der Naturforscher Goethe begreift, das wird anschaulich in den 'Lehrjahren'" [What Goethe understands as a naturalist becomes evident in the *Lehrjahre*] (9). Müller views metamorphosis as the ineluctable form of life itself, and the *Lehrjahre* as a work that exemplifies this life form. The novel both presents the development of many interwoven individual lives and develops itself in accordance with morphological principles. To the extent that the work transforms biological principles into narrative, it becomes a Bildungsroman (15; on morphological Goethe criticism see Mandelkow 1989, 97, 155).

Müller offers a good example of the continuity of literary criticism from the Third Reich into the immediate postwar period, a continuity that refutes the widespread theory of the *Kahlschlag* [a term borrowed from the practice of clear-cutting in forestry to contend that German culture and criticism made an absolute break with the past after 1945]. Müller had begun publishing morphological studies of Goethe's works as early as 1939. To be sure, he avoids using literature as propaganda by concentrating on the analysis of the literary text as a self-referential structure. This approach allowed for an appeal to an unbroken humanistic tradition even in the midst of a criminal regime. It also enabled Müller to continue his work without interruption in the immediate postwar years. Müller's apolitical criticism was perfectly suited to a generation desperate to recapture the "good" German tradition from two shameful decades of ideological abuse. As Mandelkow observes, however, Müller's morphological method has several disturbing aspects. For one thing, it is tautological, based on the premise that Goethe can best be interpreted by Goethe himself. Moreover, Müller bases his work on an image of Goethe as representing a harmonious, organic totality that stands in sharp contrast to the literary praxis of the immediate postwar era. Finally, Müller's stress on biological categories places his interpretive methodology in disturbing proximity to the racial theories of the Third Reich (Mandelkow 1989, 97-98).

Hans Heinrich Borcherdt's postwar criticism provides a particularly unsavory example of the continuity of literary criticism from the Third Reich to the early Federal Republic. Four years after the war Borcherdt published a lengthy study, *Der Roman der Goethezeit* [The Novel of the Age of Goethe] (1949). His narrative follows a familiar pattern, tracing the rise and fall of the German novel from its beginnings in the 1770s through its triumph in the 1790s to its gradual demise in the first decades of the nineteenth century. At the summit stands the Bildungsroman of the classical and romantic period represented by the novels of Jean Paul, Hölderlin, and Novalis, which are surpassed only by *Wilhelm Meisters Lehrjahre*. The hero of Goethe's Bildungsroman matures through a combination of organic growth and the pedagogical influence of the Tower Society to find self-fulfillment in an "earthly paradise" (291; see also Borcherdt 1958, 176).

At first glance, Borcherdt seems to present only a tired reformulation of the idealizing interpretation of the *Lehrjahre* that we have traced from Körner through Dilthey and beyond. Absent are the explicit appeals to Nazi racial theories that he had used in 1941 to describe the striving of the German *Volk* as represented in the Bildungsroman. By limiting his study to the "Age of Goethe," Borcherdt also removes Hans Grimm's *Volk ohne Raum* from the prominent place it had held in a trajectory that had led to the present. In a sense, however, Goethe's *Wanderjahre* takes the place formerly held by Grimm's novel as, once again, *Bildung* turns from the individual to the collective: "Um das Prinzip der Gemeinschaft dreht sich daher die Idee des Romans. Ihr soll der Einzelne mit allen seinen Kräften dienen, von ihr empfängt er das Gesetz seines Lebens" [Thus the novel turns on the concept of the community. The individual should serve it with all his energy; it legislates over his life] (577). The link between Germanness and the Bildungsroman also remains intact as the classical texts not only provide answers to the questions of the current age but also eternal solutions to the quest for the German form of life (265). Borcherdt celebrates the character Walt from Jean Paul's *Flegeljahre* [Adolescent Years] (1804-05) as the German youth who represents "eine deutsche Lebensform" that extends from *Parzival* and *Simplicissimus* to Gottfried Keller's *Der grüne Heinrich* und Wilhelm Raabe's *Der Hungerpastor* [The Hunger Pastor] (1864) (454-55). By referring to the

"German form of life" Borcherdt restores the link between biology and nationhood that had played a prominent role in his openly fascist article of 1941. On the surface, then, Borcherdt's *Der Roman der Goethezeit* takes part in the general movement to purge memories of the recent past by stressing the positive German tradition embodied in works of the "Age of Goethe." Yet Borcherdt's break with his tainted Germanistik of the Third Reich is not complete; for him, at least, 1945 seems to have marked more a slight shift of rhetoric than the degree zero of a fresh start.

Karl Schlechta's blistering refutation of pious commonplaces about *Wilhelm Meister* does represent a new point of departure for postwar Goethe studies (1953). Schlechta denies the common assumption that Meister completes his *Bildung* in the course of the *Lehrjahre* and *Wanderjahre*. Instead, the novels portray his steady decline from an initial high point. After he loses his first love, Mariane, Meister has nowhere to go but down: "Von hier ab gibt es nur Abstieg" (106). Schlechta opens his study with an analysis of the various spheres of influence Meister experiences, including Werner's prosaic business world, the socially marginal actors, and the nobility. He reserves his most bitter remarks for the members of the Tower Society. The essence of the Tower's "wisdom" can be reduced to one demand: "Gib *dein* Leben auf!" [Sacrifice *your* life!] (62). One must "learn to lose oneself in a greater mass" and "to forget oneself in dutiful activity" (61). Here Schlechta offers a thinly veiled attack on the still-recent politics of *Gleichschaltung* in the name of *Bildung*:

"Eigensinnige," Eigenbrötler, Sonderlinge jeglicher Art werden konsequent eliminiert. Wer nicht nützlicher Teil, brauchbares Werkzeug sein kann, wer sich nicht einschränken lassen will, muß ausscheiden. Wer rechtzeitig stirbt, kann von Glück sagen. (89)

["Obstinate characters," eccentrics, oddballs of every type are systematically eliminated. Those who cannot be a useful part, a serviceable tool, must be expelled. Those who die promptly can consider themselves fortunate]

He accuses the Tower Society members of a rigid and empty formalism. They strive to "annihilate fate," that is, to get everything under control, but in so doing, they sterilize the world. For Schlechta, the *Wanderjahre* becomes the negative fulfillment of the *Lehrjahre*, a social dystopia rather than the democracy envisioned by the older Thomas Mann. In its effort to assume control, the society advocates mind-numbing work, incessant wandering, and no talk of past or future. Only Montan/Jarno and Makarie stand at the periphery of this world, the former having become a sarcastic misanthrope, the latter an invalid mystic who threatens to drift into pure spirituality. Otherwise, the Tower Society manages to reduce originally full characters to shadows of their former selves.

Against this bitterly critical portrait of the Tower Society, Mignon, Philine, and the itinerant actors emerge as positive figures. Above all, Schlechta praises the young Wilhelm Meister in love with Mariane. At this stage Meister is not only a poet but is one with poetry itself. In the course of the work he gradually loses touch with this original unity, first in his critique of *Hamlet* and then when the Tower Society bleaches out his once rich character to the point that he becomes a fitting partner for the sterile Natalie. His original plenitude recurs only once in the *Wanderjahre*, in his memory of a childhood scene with a fisher boy; as Meister himself recalls, all of his subsequent experience has been a mere copy of this moment.

In the second half of his monograph Schlechta concentrates on several stylistic means by which Goethe illustrates this process of decline. His understanding of the function of the maxims included in the *Wanderjahre* is particularly valuable. Read independently, these terse sayings bear witness to Goethe's mature wisdom but within the context of the novel they serve only as a means of control, in that they reduce the complexity of the world to manageable units of packaged wisdom (168). The novellas inserted into the narrative frame of the novel retain the last remnants of healthy human interest in love and interpersonal relationships, but all are problematic, all lack the original simplicity of Meister's first love.

Until the 1970s Schlechta's work was either ignored altogether or rebuked as a willful misreading of Goethe's novels (Henkel 1955). Part of the reason lies in the historical climate in which the work was written. Schlechta's uncompromising assault on the Tower Society can only be understood as a rejection of the totalitarian government that had ruined Germany in the preceding decades. The *Germanistik* of the 1950s and early 1960s, however, sought to salvage what remained of Germany's more positive cultural legacy through a deliberately apolitical, respectful return to the classics. Thus, Schlechta's work violates the critical decorum of the period. It is important to note, however, that although Schlechta spares no scorn for the Tower Society, he never criticizes Goethe. Instead, he reads the text with meticulous care to reveal how its surface humanism and concern for *Bildung* conceals another, often frighteningly brutal world of totalitarian control. For example, he prefaces his work with a quote from Emile Montagut that begins: "Le véritable artiste est presque toujours involontairement infidèle à sa pensée première; il fait autre chose que ce qu'il voulait faire, ou il fait autrement qu'il ne voulait faire" [The true artist is almost always involuntarily unfaithful to his primary idea. He does something other than he wanted to do, or does something else that he did not want to do].

This quotation recalls Friedrich Schlegel's claim that each superior work of literature knows more that it says and intends more than it realizes (1798, 140). Schlechta's monograph can indeed be read as a work of neo-romantic criticism. Like Schlegel before him, Schlechta seeks to tease out the irony in the *Lehrjahre*, and like Novalis, he resents the increasingly prosaic nature of the text. Herein lies the primary shortcoming of Schlechta's work: namely, by viewing Meister's development in terms of a steady decline Schlechta idealizes his point of departure. Whereas most critics had followed Körner's lead and ignored the irony that marks the end of Goethe's novel, Schlechta remains blind to the irony present already at its beginning. For we as readers suspect from the outset that Mariane's involvement with Norbert will cut short Meister's moments of self-absorbed happiness (on Schlechta's Neo-Romanticism see Henkel 1955, 88; Mandelkow 1989, 174).

Thus, in the immediate postwar period Borcherdt and Schlechta stake out extreme positions regarding the interpretation of the Wilhelm Meister novels that once again fall within the boundaries established by Goethe's earliest critics but that at the same time offer encoded responses to Germany's recent past. In the ensuing decades we witness a gradual move toward Schlechta's camp in the scholarly literature on the *Lehrjahre*, as critics begin to express doubts about the nature of Meister's development, and to question the work's reputation as the prototype of the genre. In 1955 Otto Friedrich Bollnow placed the theoretical concept of *Bildung* into social-historical context. In his view Wilhelm Meister does not seek to become an *uomo universale* but attains a more limited ideal of "weltmännische Tätigkeit" [gentlemanly activity]. *Bildung* in this context refers neither to artistic nor intellectual achievement but the middle-class individual's cultivation of a personality type that enables him to move within circles with greater cultural and political power (456). From this perspective, Meister's *Bildung* is not only limited in scope but is also the product of a particular historical era, as the late eighteenth-century *Bürger* adopts a noble ideal of comportment to play a role in court society — a strategy quite familiar to Goethe himself.

Like Günther Müller, Emil Staiger develops his interpretation of the *Lehrjahre* with reference to Goethe's morphological concepts of *Bildung*. For the most part Staiger offers a conservative restatement of the view that the novel portrays the healthy growth of the protagonist toward an attainable goal (1956, 135). In his conclusion, however, Staiger expresses certain reservations about the restrictions attending the classical concept of *Bildung*. He notes, for example, how much of the world must be excluded from the novel before it reaches its happy ending, including the army, the church, and the state (168). Moreover, Wilhelm himself becomes less interesting as the novel nears its conclusion. Staiger concludes that Goethe was tired of the project and therefore finished it off with a hasty and dissatisfying ending.

After Bollnow and Staiger expressed reservations about the nature of *Bildung* portrayed in the *Lehrjahre*, Kurt May went so far as to question whether the novel deserved to be called a Bildungsroman at all. Citing Meister's letter to Werner, May notes that although Meister can describe the ideal of a rounded personality he cannot yet attain it. Hence, we can only speak of the *Lehrjahre* as a "Bildungsroman im Ansatz" [incipient Bildungsroman] (1957, 21). *Bildung* itself changes from an all-embracing, idealistic concept to a more concrete notion restricted to the point of one-sidedness (31). Any sense that Meister has completed his *Bildung* in the *Lehrjahre* is simply wrong, according to May; harmony is to be found only in the *Wanderjahre*, and here the goal of individual development has been abandoned in favor of a community of the resigned, where the previous ideal of the Bildungsroman is only touched on in passing. In short, Goethe does *not* set out to write a Bildungsroman in which the hero attains fully rounded personal development; his work must be understood as a renunciation of the neo-humanist, harmonious ideal of *Bildung* (32). Thus, the novel can in no way be viewed as espousing the ideals of Schiller's *Aesthetic Education*. In May's opinion, Goethe abandons individual striving in favor of universal harmony and advocates dedication to a particular useful activity in the service of the community.

Hans-Egon Hass's lengthy essay on the *Lehrjahre* also reflects the growing skepticism surrounding the question of Meister's development. Hass argues that error is an essential component in Wilhelm's development and that the book is guided by a pervasive sense of irony. In other words, he interprets the work much in the sense that Goethe presents Faust's development in the "Prologue in Heaven": striving is necessary, mistakes are inevitable, yet providential nature insures a positive outcome for the hero (1963, 139). Thus, Hass reduces Meister's career to a fortunate combination of coincidences rather than a personal development. Things simply happen to Wilhelm Meister; he blunders passively through life guided only by accident and the benevolent concern of the Tower Society.

Hans Eichner takes May's skepticism one step further. In Eichner's reading of the *Lehrjahre* Meister does not become a *uomo universale*, but neither does he undertake any practical activity; instead, he sets off on another journey at the end of the novel. Like Wieland's *Agathon*, the novel is about the "Ernüchterung eines Schwärmers" [disenchantment of a dreamer] (1966, 179). Hence, the society of the Tower is not meant to be utopian but realistic. In his view, Goethe portrays neither paragons of virtue nor an absolute ideal. Eichner emphasizes Goethe's awareness of the price of maturity: the process of *Bildung* involves the development of certain talents while others atrophy (191). Eichner also raises questions about the genre of the novel, pointing out that Meister might better be viewed as a picaresque character than as the hero of a Bildungsroman. Finally, Eichner counters Staiger's rather lame assertion that Goethe was in a hurry to complete his novel by claiming that Goethe deliberately wrote an operatic conclusion to underscore the unrealistic nature of the work's resolution.

Questioning the Legacy: Criticism in the 1960s

Of course, not all criticism of the Bildungsroman focused exclusively on *Wilhelm Meisters Lehrjahre* during the 1960s. Several significant studies of other German novels traditionally associated with the genre share the growing skepticism that marked the criticism of Goethe's work while offering increasingly sophisticated textual analysis. The following overview of Bildungsroman criticism of the 1960s is organized roughly in terms of the order in which the novels originally appeared.

We recall that Melitta Gerhard had extended the history of the genre by distinguishing between the structural category of the *Entwicklungsroman* and the historically specific Bildungsroman; and Fritz Martini insisted in the conclusion to his essay on Karl Morgenstern that the term *Bildungsroman* should be reserved for novels written around 1800 (1961, 263). Werner Hoffmann challenges this point of view in a 1967 essay in which he argues that Grimmelshausen's *Simplicissimus* is a Bildungsroman — but a baroque Bildungsroman! (180). In coming to this conclusion Hoffmann reverses the usual distinction between the Bildungsroman and the *Entwicklungsroman*. He finds the latter term more restricted, as it refers to biological and psychological concepts that do not apply to Grimmelshausen's work; *Bildungsroman* becomes in his view the broader, more inclusive term. *Simplicissimus* differs from the picaresque tradition by virtue of its historically specific setting in the Thirty Years War; its carefully structured composition; and its portrayal of nascent character development, revealed particularly in Simplicissimus's role as narrator. Hoffmann concedes that Grimmelshausen's protagonist does not always develop with the psychological consistency expected in works by later authors and that he rejects the world at the end of the novel. Nevertheless, Hoffmann argues that these features do not disqualify the novel as a Bildungsroman. As he points out, no single work exhibits all the characteristics of the genre. Hence, there is no reason not to consider *Simplicissimus* a Bildungsroman too, provided that we understand the text in proper historical context.

Gerda Röder follows the path blazed by Melitta Gerhard and E.L. Stahl in search of the prehistory of the Bildungsroman. She investigates what she terms the narrative possibilities of the plausible realization of *Glück* [happiness or good fortune] in works ranging from the baroque novel to *Wilhelm Meisters Wanderjahre* (1968, 20). Not surprisingly, she discovers a gradual trend toward secularization. Fortune changes from an external force in an unstable world in the baroque novel to a personal achievement on the part of the hero; happiness initially conceived in terms of a rejection of this world gradually yields to the attempt to find satisfaction here and now. Johann Gottfried Schnabel's *Die Insel Felsenburg* [Felsenburg Island] (1731-43) marks an early stage in this process, as Schnabel values human self-determination and depicts an attempt to found a utopian community on earth. Happiness comes only from within for Wieland's Agathon; conflicts caused by external fate turn to inner struggles in the mind of the enthusiast. The problem of narration becomes increasingly important, for the ending of the novel must be rendered plausible to the reader. Thus, we view the outcome of Agathon's adventures through the critical eyes of the ironic narrator. In Goethe's *Lehrjahre* the concept of happiness has become completely internalized and is specific to different characters. The novel as a whole portrays happiness as an understanding that can embrace both Mignon's tragedy and Wilhelm's comedy: "So liegt die Harmonie ... nicht in der Ausklammerung allen Unglücks, sondern in der kunstvollen Verflechtung von Glück und Unglück, welche das tragische Schicksal als solches bestehen läßt" [Thus harmony lies ... not in the exclusion of all unhappiness, but rather in the artistic interweaving of happiness and unhappiness which leaves the tragic fate as such intact] (181).

In this way Röder steers a course between what she views as simplistically positive (Borcherdt) or overly negative (Schlechta) readings of Goethe's novel. In doing so, however, Röder employs a dialectical sleight of hand to avoid the popular misconception that the Bildungsroman brings its hero to bliss in an earthly paradise. Röder defines true happiness for Goethe as something that always already includes unhappiness in an attempt to preserve the sense of accomplishment granted the protagonist at the novel's conclusion without minimizing the extent of his suffering. Her work therefore reflects contemporary uneasiness with the Bildungsroman while complementing the earlier studies by Gerhard and Stahl. Röder develops an intelligent survey of changing concepts of *Glück* in German novels during the greater eighteenth century; having brought her narrative up to Goethe, however, she, like both previous critics, stops. The question of whether or not an investigation of the concept of happiness would yield useful insights into novels of the next two centuries remains unanswered.

Like Werner Hoffmann, François Jost adopts a pragmatic attitude toward the question of genre in his article "La Tradition du 'Bildungsroman'" (1969). Noting the tendency toward taxonomic proliferation in studies of the novel and its subgenres, he reminds us that any given text will partake of various traditions. We should conceive of genre as a fluid category, not a rigid scheme that cuts off further discussion. Although Jost views the Bildungsroman as a predominantly German genre he is willing to consider related works in other European national literatures, and he lists many examples. He is particularly interested in the relation of the French novel to the German Bildungsroman and discusses both Stendhal's autobiographical novel *Vie de Henri Brulard* (1831-1939) and Rousseau's *Emile* in this context. His treatment of the latter as a Bildungsroman breaks with the commonly held view that *Emile* is a typical *Erziehungsroman*, a didactic work in which a mentor leads a student to a predetermined goal. As Jost reminds us, Rousseau's concept of education works differently: "qu'au lieu *d'éduquer* l'enfant, il faut lui permettre de *s'éduquer* lui-même" [instead of educating the child, one must permit him to educate himself] (113). Precisely this concept of education informs the Tower Society's conscious decision *not* to interfere with the course of Wilhelm Meister's life, suggesting that the two works have more in common than is generally assumed.

Jost's wide-ranging essay covers much familiar ground for the Germanist; but as an article written in French and published in an American journal of comparative literature, it addresses a broader audience. His work also anticipates two trends that will develop in subsequent decades. First, *Germanistik* becomes increasingly international. Many important studies of the German Bildungsroman have been written by non-Germans in recent decades, particularly in English-speaking countries. Second, Jost takes the term formerly identified with either German spiritual essence or Germany's troubled political history and applies it to the study of other national literatures.

Lawrence Ryan's subtle interpretation of Friedrich Hölderlin's *Hyperion* (1797-99), while not explicitly concerned with the theory of the Bildungsroman, nevertheless combines an attentiveness to both the philosophy of *Bildung* and problems of narration that will preoccupy subsequent critics of the genre. The eponymous hero of Hölderlin's novel lives in modern Greece. In a series of letters to a friend in Germany he recalls his childhood and youth, his experiences in love and war, and finally a trip to Germany that leaves him horrified at its cultural and moral degeneracy. Ryan argues that Hölderlin presents a double development in his novel: the first is that of Hyperion's growth to adulthood; the second, and ultimately the more important one, involves his role as narrator. The resulting work does not present lyric immediacy in the tradition of Goethe's *Werther*; instead, the text becomes a site of self-reflexive interiority ("der auf sich selber *reflektierenden* Innerlichkeit") (1965, 4). The narrator repeats and eventually surpasses the development of the protagonist: "In der erzählerischen Reflexion wird somit das durchgehende Entwicklungsprinzip des Romans in potenzierter Form wiederholt" [Thus, the novel's continuous principle of development is repeated at a higher power in the narrative reflection] (6).

Ryan specifies the nature of Hyperion's development by using Hölderlin's concept of the eccentric path (*exzentrische Bahn*). Development begins when individual consciousness tears itself loose from its direct connection to Being (*zum Seinsganzen*). What follows is a series of oscillations between the eccentric path of the individual away from the center of Being and periodic recenterings around the self (*Selbstzentrierung*). Yet the new self-centeredness of the individual no longer partakes of the original belonging-to-Being (*Seinszugehörigkeit*). If the alienated self is to achieve the desired reconciliation with nature, this solipsistic moment cannot last. Thus, nature steps in periodically to correct (*zurechtweisen*) the centrifugal striving of the self away from the center. Nevertheless, the eccentric path soon asserts its force again (12-14).

Left at this stage, the self would not so much develop as eternally oscillate between fleeting moments of ecstatic unity with nature and renewed awareness of its alienation from nature. Nature itself, however, steps out of its unity with Being when it enters into time (156). Herein lies the key to the "'Auflösung der Dissonanzen'" [resolution of dissonances] in the novel (223), for the very temporality that drives Hyperion away from a primal unity with God-Nature can now be perceived as the unity of the transient self with divine nature in the process of becoming. Now the sense of suffering and loss that accompanies the temporal self can be affirmed as part of nature: "das Leiden wird nun zur Bedingung alles Wechsels und Werdens, auch in der Natur" [suffering now becomes the prerequisite of all change and growth, also in nature] (223). To be sure, Hyperion himself does not attain this perspective at the end of the novel, which could lead to the impression that he remains trapped in a vicious circle. But the narrator does, and Ryan's argument is that the real end of the novel comes when the retrospective narrator learns to affirm nature's suffering. Hyperion as narrator completes the process of *Bildung* he leaves unfinished as a character.

One might object that Ryan imposes an overly schematic and overly optimistic philosophical structure onto a novel that remains formally fragmented, socially critical, and painfully alienated from the divine nature it seeks. Nevertheless, his sophisticated discussion of *Hyperion* anticipates two developments in the study of the genre. First, like Röder, he defines the goal of *Bildung* in such a way that it includes an acceptance of pain as well as happiness. Second, Ryan signals an increased attentiveness to narrative consciousness in the Bildungsroman.

While many critics of the early twentieth century had stressed the continuity of the German tradition of the Bildungsroman from Goethe to their own time, many in the 1960s began to underscore the differences between the nineteenth-century novel and the classical heritage. In 1962, for example, Fritz Martini emphasized Adalbert Stifter's experience of the 1848 revolution as a central impulse for his aesthetic production. Horrified by the tumultuous events of contemporary history, Stifter sought to create in *Der Nachsommer* an aesthetic order that enables us to glimpse an eternal divine world through a transfigured reality. In the *Lehrjahre*, *Bildung* had involved the interaction of the protagonist with the world as life experiences shape the developing individual. In contrast, *Bildung* in *Der Nachsommer* is no longer a subjective individual process but an objectifying experience that leads to the perception of typical life forms (519). Stifter's religiously motivated aesthetics also evidence a reverence for the culture of Germany's classical period, as he finds his typical forms in the poetry of the past. From this perspective, *Bildung* involves the acquisition of a preexistent cultural property (*Kulturgut*). Stifter inherits, organizes, and reassembles the classical heritage; his work stands on the border of a new bourgeois relation to art that stresses the caretaking of the cultural inheritance rather than the active production of something new (523).

In the following year Walther Killy stressed continuity over change when he insisted that *Der Nachsommer* should be regarded as the quintessential Bildungsroman, "der Bildungsroman schlechthin" (1963, 84). At a time when other European novelists were producing critical depictions of social reality, Stifter writes a work in deliberate opposition to his historical situation. Poignantly aware of his position at the end of Germany's classical period, Stifter constructs a nostalgic, conservative utopia. At the same time, Victor Lange contested the common view that *Der Nachsommer* should be considered a Bildungsroman (1963). The topic of the novel, in his view, is not Heinrich Drendorf's development, but the tale of renunciation in the lives of Risach and Mathilde. By voluntarily relinquishing their love for one another, the members of the older generation offer an example of virtue and reason triumphing over passion. *Der Nachsommer* is therefore less about individual growth than about the process of sublimation and sacrifice. He does not conceive his characters as realistic psychological portraits; rather, they represent idealized types who reveal the divinely sanctioned, eternal order of the world. Lange concludes that Stifter's novel is closer in spirit to Goethe's late "Novelle" (1828) than to the *Lehrjahre;* in it he advocates not so much a flight from reality as a melancholy recognition of the need for resignation.

Horst Albert Glaser turns even more sharply away from Killy's reading of Stifter's *Nachsommer* in an interpretation schooled on Theodor Adorno's aesthetic theory (1965). Whereas previous critics had stressed Stifter's ambition to reveal an eternal religious order, Glaser views Stifter's novel as response to the rapid industrialization of Austrian society and the rise of the bourgeoisie to a position of economic and political power. Although the novel was written in a particular sociopolitical context, Glaser argues, the world depicted in it should not be confused with realism. Landscape features as a beautiful panorama, an idealized sphere far removed from the alienated life of the Austrian city-dwellers. As such it functions as a projection of middle-class desires rather than as an objective representation of reality (7). Glaser also stresses the difference between Stifter's novel and the classical Bildungs-roman. In *Wilhelm Meisters Lehrjahre* Goethe postulates an idealized harmony between subjective desires and objective reality, whereas Stifter's characters lack all psychological depth (18). Love loses its inwardness in Stifter's novel and becomes mere convention, a social ritual (25). It is in Stifter's reduction of his characters to cardboard cutouts that Glaser sees the highest form of irony in *Der Nachsommer*. The very emptiness of the figures who come together in the utopian aesthetic world reveals the irresolvable problems of reality and prevents the novel from slipping into a sickly-sweet glorification of middle-class life (27). At other times, however, Glaser is less willing to absolve Stifter of the charge of ideology. He refers to the idealized landscapes in the novel as a compensatory pleasure that distracts from existing social problems (14). Elsewhere he writes of the "despotism of the idyll" (53) that excludes work and poverty from its domain and reduces the exploited working classes to window-dressings for the leisured rich. In his "restoration utopia" Stifter creates a "Pensionopolis" (56), a retirement community of the leisure class where all signs of social suffering have been carefully removed from view.

Gottfried Keller's *Der grüne Heinrich* also underwent renewed scrutiny during this period. In 1963 Wolfgang Preisendanz began his discussion of the novel by acknowledging that critics had begun to doubt the truism that it represented *the* Bildungsroman of German Poetic Realism. He nevertheless adopts this formula as his point of departure to specify the difference between this text and its Goethean counterpart. For Preisendanz, Keller does not depict a process of development centering on the interaction between innate talent and the environment or between nature and education. Keller's primary interest lies in the realm of perception, or more specifically, in the role of the imagination in mediating between inner and outer reality (101). As a youth Heinrich finds it difficult to distinguish between fantasy and reality, a difficulty reflected both in his painting and in his relations with women. The problem continues in slightly different form in the second part of the novel. Here Heinrich is caught between self-love and the demands of the world as he exploits his mother to sustain himself. The result is a tragic combination of maturity and guilt (104-05). Here again it is the narrator who manages to overcome the dilemma that overwhelms the protagonist. What Preisendanz terms "humoristic inwardness" enables Keller to establish a balance between poetic interiority and prosaic reality in a narrative perspective that hovers in an ironic distance from the individuals and events portrayed. By reconciling the demands of the poetic imagination with the facticity of the external world, moreover, Keller solves the central problem of Poetic Realism (110).

Hartmut Laufhütte's study of *Der grüne Heinrich* also reflects both in-creased interest in narration in the Bildungsroman and growing discomfort with the term itself (1969). Laufhütte argues that the concepts of the *Entwicklungsroman* and Bildungsroman reflect a Goethean faith in the possi-bility of individual development in a benevolent universe (352-53). Although Laufhütte concedes that Keller structures his novel around one individual, he contends that it portrays anything but the harmonious development of the protagonist. Heinrich Lee neither thrives like a plant nor takes charge of his life through an active assertion of the will. Accidents and other forces beyond his control assert their power over him (355). Keller's novel could only be considered as the negation of the classical genre, whether it be conceived as a Bildungsroman, an *Entwicklungsroman*, or an *Erziehungsroman* (356-58). Laufhütte attributes this negation to the influence of Ludwig Feuerbach's materialist philosophy. Keller lacks Goethe's faith in a transcendent perspec-tive that assures a positive outcome for the wandering character. In Goethe's worldview no experiences are lost; everything contributes to the molding of the harmonious individual. For Keller, in contrast, lost time is gone for good: mistakes cannot be corrected, and guilt is irrevocable (356-57). The loss of a divine perspective that renders individual development impossible affects the narrative form of Keller's novel as well. His tendency to build his work out of separate episodes should not be viewed as evidence of his inability to compose a novel but as a way of demonstrating the random course of the individual's life by juxtaposing it with equally accidental fates. It is up to the reader to compare and contrast different characters in the productive reception of the work, a process Laufhütte refers to with the Goethean concept of "repeated mirroring" (361). The narrative technique is the adequate reflection of Keller's lost faith in a transcendent perspective.

Laufhütte pays particular attention to the distinction between the protago-nist's dual role as a failed painter and as the successful narrator of his autobi-ography. Keller employs a third-person narrator in the first published version of his novel (1854-55). Into this frame he inserts Heinrich's account of his childhood and youth, which takes up more than half of the entire novel. In the revised version of 1879-80 Keller maintains the first-person narration throughout. At the end of the original autobiography Keller signals a break; the rest of the novel is narrated by the much older Heinrich Lee, who returns to "wander the green paths of memory again"—something that would have been impossible for the hero of the original version in any case, as he dies miserably on returning to his Swiss home.

Laufhütte argues that Heinrich Lee's reflections after spending forty days and forty nights reading Goethe's complete works serve as the organizing center of the novel (347). The narrator identifies two aspects of the Goethean aesthetic: the ability to observe reality from a distanced perspective and a willingness to enter into the service of the community. Objective observation leads to ethical commitment. The aspiring painter Heinrich Lee fails on both counts: his art remains merely subjective, a fantastic retreat from reality, and it ensnares him in guilt toward his mother and the community after a series of wasted years in Munich. Yet the same character who fails as a painter has more success as a narrator. The younger autobiographer already displays some critical distance from his blundering attempts to become an artist, whereas the older narrator provides a detached account of his futile efforts to become a painter. Here Laufhütte comes close to turning Keller's novel into a Bildungsroman after all. In the act of composing his autobiography Heinrich has the opportunity to overcome the lost orientation of a world without transcendence through the ordered creation of an organic work of art (374). As in Lawrence Ryan's study of *Hyperion*, the *Bildung* denied the protagonist as a character resurfaces in his role as narrator.

The hesitancy on the part of many critics to extend the term *Bildungsroman* to nineteenth-century German novels grew even more acute in studies of Thomas Mann's twentieth-century fiction. Whereas Hermann Weigand had once confidently inserted *Der Zauberberg* into an unbroken tradition that led back to Goethe, Erich Heller argues that Mann's novel represents an ironic reversal of the Bildungsroman convention (1958, 213), and Theodore Ziolkowski goes so far as to term it a travesty of the genre (1969, 89). It is within this context that Jürgen Scharfschwerdt sets out to reassess the relation between Thomas Mann and the German Bildungsroman (1967). Scharfschwerdt understands Mann's oeuvre as a hermeneutic process in which he seeks to engage specific problems of his own changing historical situation by adapting and developing the literary tradition. He surveys most of Mann's major works from *Buddenbrooks* to *Felix Krull* but pays particular attention to *Der Zauberberg* as both a parody and a renewal of the Bildungsroman.

Scharfschwerdt begins by acknowledging the common consensus that Mann alludes to the traditional Bildungsroman: previous critics all note the central role played by Hans Castorp, his prolonged exposure to varied pedagogical influences on the mountaintop, and the unabashed message of the "Schnee" chapter. As Scharfschwerdt observes, however, Castorp does not develop in the course of the novel; if anything, he becomes increasingly irresponsible and detached. The seemingly pivotal vision in the snow brings no noticeable change in character, and it occurs long before the novel's end. Scharfschwerdt concludes that the novel is not about the *Bildung* of an individual hero (119). What kind of novel is it, then? He points out first that it contains elements of the *Zeitroman:* it diagnoses the intellectual malaise of prewar Europe from the perspective of the Weimar Republic. Scharfschwerdt goes on to reconceive the protagonist's function within this context. In his view, Castorp plays a central role as a mediator between the various one-

sided opinions presented in the novel. As he himself does not develop, however, it is up to the reader to continue the process of *Bildung* he began and
to translate the abstract ideal into historical reality (161). In this way Scharfschwerdt salvages the failure of *Bildung* in *Der Zauberberg* by transferring
it to the reader. Given both the highly uncertain conclusion of the novel itself
and the subsequent course of German history, one must question whether this
interpretive sleight of hand does justice to either the text or its reception.

T.J. Reed confronts the skeptics head-on when he says unequivocally that
Der Zauberberg "is a *Bildungsroman* in good earnest" (1974, 226). In Reed's
opinion, Mann states his theme baldly in the "Schnee" chapter: "Indeed, for
all his subtlety Thomas Mann is simpler here than his critics are sometimes
prepared to believe. The clear-cut allegory was meant to be read as a clear-
cut allegory" (254). Reed nevertheless must come to terms with the problems
that vexed previous critics, including Scharfschwerdt: if the italicized admoni-
tion to Hans Castorp that he subordinate his fascination with death to an
affirmation of life indeed constitutes the novel's "message," why does it not
come closer to the end of the novel, why does Castorp forget it almost immediately, and why does the novel conclude with him running toward near-
certain death on the battlefields of World War I? Reed resolves this interpretive dilemma by reaching outside the text for evidence offered by the history
of the novel's composition. He recalls that Mann first conceived of *Der
Zauberberg* as a comic counterpart to *Der Tod in Venedig* [Death in Venice]
(1913). It could only become a Bildungsroman after Mann had completed his
own education from political conservative to advocate of the Weimar Republic. With this background in mind, Reed argues that Mann allows Castorp to
anticipate his own positive insight of 1924 in the dream; when Castorp forgets
the dream he falls back into Mann's discredited pre-war position (263). The
temporal gap between the historical situation depicted in the novel and
Mann's point of view when completing it allows Castorp to function as "both
the bearer of a message and the object of criticism" (262). Reed later suggests
that the discrepancy between the unequivocal message of the "Schnee" chapter and the novel's ambivalent conclusion reflects "the dilemma of an artist
who wishes both to remain an artist and to influence the world outside art"
(274). In both cases Reed puts his finger on plausible sources for the awk-
wardness many readers have felt in coming to terms with Mann's effort to
reinvent the Bildungsroman in the 1920s. The recent convert to democracy
offers a heartfelt testimonial to his new faith, while the conservative artist
does his best to muddle the message.

While critics were beginning to question the relation of canonical texts by
Goethe, Stifter, Keller, and Mann to the Bildungsroman, novelists continued
to produce works that seemed to continue the tradition. This is the case for
what is perhaps the most celebrated postwar German novel, Günter Grass's

Die Blechtrommel [The Tin Drum] (1959). Grass himself maintained in interviews that his novel stood in an "ironically distanced relation to the German Bildungsroman" (Neuhaus 1979, 38). It is the familiar story of Oskar Matzerath, a boy born fully conscious into prewar Danzig who voluntarily stunts his growth at age three. From this perspective he watches the Nazis assume power, experiences the war and its aftermath, and finally composes his life history while incarcerated in a sanatorium. Reduced to this outline, Grass's novel hardly seems a likely candidate for the German genre. Yet one of the most influential early readers of *Die Blechtrommel* immediately signaled its place in literary history in an essay entitled "Wilhelm Meister, auf Blech getrommelt" [Wilhelm Meister, Drummed on Tin] (1959). Hans Magnus Enzensberger states his point directly: *"Die Blechtrommel* ist ein Entwicklungs- und Bildungsroman" (11). In making this claim Enzensberger stresses the distance between Grass's novel and contemporary experimental fiction. Grass composes his novel with a technical virtuosity that leaves no detail superfluous, no threads untied. To this extent *Die Blechtrommel* recalls the classics and almost seems old-fashioned today. Yet is it precisely Grass's objectivity that enables him to portray the Hitler regime for what it was: the incarnation of shabby filth devoid of any demonic grandeur (10). Grass also refutes those eager to proclaim the death of the novel, the end of plot, and the dissolution of characters. Yet his seemingly traditional narrative does not simply repeat the classical genre of the Bildungsroman. Grass makes use of the tradition but at the same time undercuts and rejects it. Like Wilhelm Meister and Heinrich Lee before him, Oskar Matzerath is a child of his century: a drummer, a cripple, and an idiot (12; on specific links to the *Lehrjahre* in terms of both characters and plot motifs see Cunliffe 1969; for a more recent overview of critical opinion on the relation of *Die Blechtrommel* to the genre of the Bildungsroman see Krumme 1986, 74-80).

Taking Stock: Köhn and Jacobs Survey the Bildungsroman

Lothar Köhn's 1969 survey of Bildungsroman criticism offers a careful summary of what had become an enormous body of secondary literature on the topic. He begins by sifting through the various and often contradictory ways in which the terms *Bildungsroman* and *Entwicklungsroman* have been used and comes to the tentative conclusion that the latter term generally refers to a suprahistorical structural type, whereas the Bildungsroman is the product of the era of Goethe (8-9). Köhn remains basically undogmatic in his understanding of the Bildungsroman, noting that the very openness of the genre's definition has made it particularly useful as a hermeneutic tool (78). He concludes that we might as well continue to use the term, as long as nothing better takes its place (87).

Köhn notes the persistent tendency to view the Bildungsroman as something peculiarly German, a phenomenon that leads to either "ideological valorization" or to its complete discredit among readers. He remains properly critical of those who have abused the category for ideological purposes, particularly during the 1930s and 1940s. Köhn himself appeals for further "typological" analyses of the novels' structure, along the lines of Franz Stanzel, Eberhard Lämmert, and Wolfgang Kayser (9-15, 88). He also calls for further analyses of the utopian aspects of the genre. In conclusion, Köhn laments the generally low quality of Bildungsroman scholarship and calls for a history of the entire genre. Within three years Jürgen Jacobs was to supply what Köhn had sought.

The increasingly critical tendency we have traced in the postwar reception of the *Lehrjahre* finds its fullest expression in Jürgen Jacobs's study of the genre as a whole, *Wilhelm Meister und seine Brüder* [Wilhelm Meister and His Brothers] (1972). Whereas previous authors had restricted their attention to Goethe's novel and perhaps a handful of related texts, Jacobs treats dozens of works written since the mid eighteenth century. In addition, he includes excursuses on related works of philosophy (Hegel's *Phänomenologie*) and criticism (Blanckenburg's *Versuch über den Roman*), and a brief sketch of the novel in England and France. Like many previous critics, Jacobs considers the Bildungsroman a peculiarly German tradition, but with a crucial difference: he replaces vague appeals to national essence with careful references to the concrete historical circumstances that gave rise to this type of novel in Germany.

Jacobs argues that the Bildungsroman is the product of the optimistic mentality of the rising middle class in eighteenth-century Germany. Ideally the genre portrays individual maturation culminating in a resolution of dissonance symbolized by the integration of the hero into society. He views the stress on inwardness in the German tradition as a reflection of the political backwardness of Germany vis-à-vis France and England. As a result, the desired reconciliation between the individual and society can never convincingly take place. Hence, the genre remains "unfulfilled" (271); his study reveals that the irresolvable nature of its fundamental question always becomes evident and that the genre can therefore never achieve the inner closure it seeks (54).

Jacobs finds evidence of this problem even in *Wilhelm Meisters Lehrjahre*, which he views as the paradigm of the genre. He succinctly and convincingly debunks several previous readings of the text: the Tower Society does not guide Meister to higher maturity; rather, its basic pedagogical principle is to leave individual development up to chance. Nor does Meister develop like a plant in accordance with Goethe's morphological theories, as Müller and Staiger had argued; nor does Meister himself take charge of his *Bildung* through an act of will. Rather, Goethe brings his hero to a surprisingly happy ending through an optimistic belief that things will turn out for the best, *despite* the hero's passivity, provided that he maintain the "'Wille zur Ausbildung'" [desire to develop] that his friend Werner lacks (83). Successful *Bildung* for Goethe involves a recognition of limitations, a self-imposed restriction of ambition. Moreover, Jacobs recognizes the role of irony in Goethe's text, evident particularly in the novel's conclusion. As Friedrich Schlegel had argued, the book anticipates its own critique, and it is precisely this ironic qualification of the novel's happy ending that makes it typical of the genre as a whole (89).

Despite this claim, Jacobs spends most of his time proving that individual novels are *not* examples of the Bildungsroman. His argument takes two basic forms, one synchronic, one diachronic. He works out the first argument in his brief consideration of Hegel's *Phänomenologie*, which he views as a philosophical pendant to the literary genre of the Bildungsroman (105). Here he argues that the Bildungsroman falls short of its ideal in one of two ways: novels either offer utopian solutions that leave reality behind or demonstrate the necessary failure of the project of *Bildung* in a given social setting. The works of the German Romantics, in particular Novalis's *Heinrich von Ofterdingen*, provide good examples of the first tendency, one that continues in Adalbert Stifter's *Nachsommer*, Hermann Hesse's *Siddhartha* (1922), and — with increasingly disturbing ideological tendencies—in Hans Grimm's *Volk ohne Raum*. At the opposite extreme lie those *Desillusionsromane* that end in dissonance or despair; prominent examples include Karl Philipp Moritz's *Anton Reiser* (1785-90), E.T.A. Hoffmann's *Lebensansichten des Katers Murr*, Keller's *Der grüne Heinrich*, and Günter Grass's *Die Blechtrommel*. Jacobs combines this negative dialectic with a historical narrative that can be reduced to a simple opposition between not yet and no longer — that is, novels that precede and follow *Wilhelm Meisters Lehrjahre*.

It is therefore not surprising when Jacobs concludes that the Bildungsroman is an "unfulfilled genre." His concept of the Bildungsroman functions as a Platonic category most useful as a diagnostic tool that reveals the unresolved discord in particular texts. This approach makes his study both extremely valuable for the analysis of individual works and disappointing for its depiction of the genre as a whole. His persistent skepticism cuts through platitudes about the quintessentially German genre; at the same time, however, he effectively dismantles the genre itself by reducing it to one novel, itself acutely aware of the tentative nature of its resolution.

If we step outside the troubling logic of Jacobs's study, additional problems emerge. The very scope of his work gives the impression that he has produced a thorough analysis of the German novel. In fact, however, he restricts his attention to the accepted canon, ignoring German social novels, popular fiction, and all texts by women writers. We are left, then, with a seemingly exhaustive list of canonical texts chosen primarily because they seem to be, but finally are *not* Bildungsromane; other works have no place at all in German literary history. Nevertheless, Jacobs's achievement should not be ignored. He sums up an increasingly skeptical attitude toward the German Bildungsroman with perceptive analysis of individual texts, and while his views on the genre as a whole will provoke rebuttals, the work remains a benchmark of Bildungsroman scholarship.

Reception Theory and Ideology Critique in the 1970s

The advent of German reception theory in the 1970s signaled a paradigm shift in the presuppositions governing literary analysis. Literary criticism no longer seemed an objective science in the pursuit of hard facts. Interpretive models change in the course of history, critics observed, and present concerns motivate the investigation of the past. Thus, attention shifted away from the text and toward the reader in Wolfgang Iser's phenomenological investigations of the act of reading and in Hans Robert Jauß's focus on the role of reception in the making of literary history. Jauß's influence, in particular, led to a radical historicization of literary studies as critics began to question the ideological function of particular beliefs a given society. This willingness to question the authority of Germany's classical heritage coincided with the student revolts throughout Europe and North America in the late 1960s and early 1970s. In Germany this spirit of protest brought about a belated attempt to come to terms with the Nazi past that had been repressed by the older generation. Given the close historical connection between the emergence of the Bildungsroman into critical discourse and the development of Germany into a world power, it is not surprising that the genre came under sharp scrutiny during this period (on the cultural significance of reception theory in Germany see Holub 1984, 1-12).

Klaus F. Gille's *"Wilhelm Meister" im Urteil der Zeitgenossen* ["Wilhelm Meister" in the Opinion of its Contemporaries] (1971) belongs to the first wave of the reception theory that swept Germany in the 1970s. Gille begins by questioning the notion that our understanding of literary texts is objective and timeless. He distrusts shopworn descriptions of the *Lehrjahre* as the "classical German Bildungsroman" (4) and undertakes to examine this thesis in the light of the novel's early reception. One of Gille's primary achievements is to demonstrate how the divergent opinions of the novel's first readers helped shape subsequent debates about it. By placing Goethe's work in the historical context of its reception, Gille complicates the teleology that had dominated most previous studies of Weimar Classicism in general and the Bildungsroman in particular. What in retrospect seemed a natural ripening of German literature toward its fruition in the works of Goethe and Schiller suddenly appears as the conscious achievement of two isolated individuals. Gille points out that Weimar Classicism coincides with the late Enlightenment, early Romanticism, and even remnants of mid-century *Empfindsamkeit* [sentimentality], which reveals the narrow basis of support for the representatives of German Classicism (5). Goethe's novel was *not* universally recognized as the "classical German Bildungsroman" at the time it appeared: opinions ranged from Körner's rose-glass reading through Novalis's love-hate reaction to the work to the majority of readers who lamented that Goethe had not produced another *Werther*. Gille's work signals a reversal in German literary history: nineteenth-century canon formation resulted in a drastic reduction in the number of texts preserved for study and as the record of the unfolding German *Geist*, whereas the reception theorist resituates the canonical work among its many contemporary literary rivals and recalls the conflicting critical opinions it first provoked.

While Gille reevaluated the beginnings of the Bildungsroman, Georg Just brought the insights of contemporary theory to bear on a more recent addition to the literary tradition (1972). Just focuses on the production of meaning generated in the reader by Grass's *Die Blechtrommel*. He begins with a simple question: is the novel critical? By "critical" Just means a text that breaks with what Jauß terms the reader's "horizon of expectations" to generate awareness of the subjective, perspectival view of the world we generally mistake for objective truth. In becoming alert to the presuppositions that structure our world, we have the potential to change them. Here Just draws on Iser's phenomenology of reading; at the same time, he supplements reception aesthetics with historical analysis of the novel's content in an effort to move beyond the identification of gaps (*Leerstellen*) in the text (31-32).

Just argues that Grass establishes the horizon of expectation in *Die Blechtrommel* primarily by aligning it with the tradition of the Bildungsroman. He bases his understanding of the genre on Lukács's *Theory of the Novel*, where the Bildungsroman is introduced as an attempted solution to the problem of transcendental homelessness in the modern age. *Wilhelm Meisters Lehrjahre* leads to the reconciliation of the individual with society, reflecting a belief in evolutionary change and progress toward an ideal. Later in the nineteenth century Wilhelm Raabe writes novels about outsiders who resign themselves from meaningful participation in society. In Just's view, Oskar Matzerath differs significantly from both the evolving eighteenth-century protagonist and his alienated nineteenth-century counterpart in that he lacks all interiority. He is not an individual in the same sense as the earlier figures;

he functions as the embodiment of a particular perspective that guides the reader's activity (90). Because Oskar cannot formulate a critique of his society, the reader must assume this task. What the reader perceives, according to Just, is the link between political terror and the resolutely apolitical behavior of private citizens. That is, the novel grants its readers insight into the catastrophic consequences of the petit-bourgeois refusal to recognize their complicity in the criminal acts of the fascist state. The very negation of explicit meaning in the text inspires its readers to revolutionary consciousness (218), and for this reason Just argues that art is the best instrument of ideology critique (36). In conclusion, however, he does acknowledge that readers may not notice the implicit conflict in the text and may therefore fail to realize its critical potential (228).

As interest grew in the history of literary criticism and the reception of particular authors, critics also became increasingly concerned with the way in which the writers themselves addressed contemporary issues in their literary works. Giuliano Baioni's interpretation of *Wilhelm Meisters Lehrjahre* provides a good example of this approach (1975). The Italian critic interprets the *Lehrjahre* as Goethe's response to the French Revolution, a response that offers, as a conservative alternative to political chaos, an alliance between the German middle class and an enlightened nobility. Baioni views the novel's conclusion as the utopian formulation of a historical compromise: the bourgeoisie sacrifices its political desires to achieve its ethical and aesthetic ideals within the context of a modest reform of the existing order (109).

Rolf-Peter Janz adopts a similar strategy in his analysis of the social content of the *Lehrjahre* (1975). Janz argues that we should not view this content as a direct reflection of Goethe's immediate surroundings but as an ideally typical aesthetic model of a society constituted by four separate groups: the middle class, the theater troupe, a frivolous Rococo nobility, and a progressive, reformed nobility (320-21). The novel portrays the difficulties confronting the bourgeois individual who seeks self-realization in a feudal society. While the life of the nobility entices Wilhelm Meister, the progressive nobles of the Tower Society realize that their future lies in adopting the attitudes of the bourgeoisie, particularly regarding the wise investment of capital. Thus, the seemingly universal appeal of the humanistic *Bildungsideal* in Goethe's novel becomes the basis for overcoming the opposition between the bourgeoisie and the nobility.

Gerhard Mayer turns away from the Goethe's *Lehrjahre* to investigate the alternative tradition of the Antibildungsroman (1974). Summing up the current mood, Mayer observes that the venerable genre that once seemed to offer a timeless standard in the classical concept of *Bildung* now appears as the questionable product of a society so frightened of anarchic subjectivity that it was willing to subordinate individual desires to collective utility (1974,

41-2). In their extreme reaction to the Goethean prototype, the early German Romantics left social reality behind in novels that portray the poetically transfigured subjectivity of isolated heroes. Against these two opposing prototypes Mayer develops his concept of the Antibildungsroman. The sub- or countergenre emerges out of a healthy skepticism regarding a given society's ideal of *Bildung* and exposes its weaknesses or limitations (43). Mayer discusses four examples of the Antibildungsroman: Jean Paul's *Flegeljahre*, Hoffmann's *Kater Murr*, Raabe's *Stopfkuchen* (1891), and Grass's *Die Blechtrommel*.

Mayer's use of the term *Antibildungsroman* marks the beginning of a popular trend. The concept enables critics to signal that a particular novel participates in a recognized literary tradition and at the same time to disassociate the text from the conservative ideology associated with the genre's history. Mayer's essay also illustrates one of the main shortcomings of this approach: in developing the notion of a socially critical Antibildungsroman he oversimplifies the Bildungsroman. He uses *Wilhelm Meisters Lehrjahre* as a straw man to introduce the allegedly more problematic novels that follow, thereby ignoring a growing body of literature that had begun to question the accuracy of earlier affirmative readings of Goethe's text. Teleology also plays an uncertain role in Mayer's argument. He insists in his conclusion that the Antibildungsroman does not develop *after* the Bildungsroman but accompanies the primary genre from its inception: "Kritik und Zweifel an der modernen, im 18. Jahrhundert entstandenen Bildungsidee sind so alt wie diese selbst" [Critique and doubt of the modern concept of Bildung that arose in the eighteenth century are as old as the concept itself] (61). Nevertheless, Mayer frequently describes a pattern of progressive historical decline. The poetic synthesis of the early romantic novel is "no longer possible" for E.T.A. Hoffmann (47), society can no longer offer positive values to Raabe's hero, and Grass's Antibildungsroman portrays "the impossibility of a human existence in an inhuman society" (58). In short: the Antibildungsroman functions as a useful heuristic device in illuminating discussions of nonclassical texts. The theoretical weakness of the argument lies in the pallid image of the Bildungsroman that remains.

Monika Schrader's study of *mimesis* and *poiesis* in the Bildungsroman (1975) marks a departure from the widespread interest in reception theory during the 1970s. She begins by rejecting the predominantly content-oriented focus of previous studies and proposes instead to investigate the structural principles of the Bildungsroman. Schrader identifies Wieland's *Agathon* as the first Bildungsroman and devotes the first half of her book to its analysis. As Blanckenburg had stressed, the significance of external events in Wieland's novel lies solely in their relation to the inner development of the protagonist. Schrader argues that greater subjectivity on the part of the protagonist carries over to the role of the narrator. The narrator changes from the passive medium through which we view objective reality to a creative presence who shapes our perception of the world. Self-consciousness on the part of the hero takes the form of narrative self-consciousness. The emergence of the Bildungsroman is the story of its narrative form. *Bildung* consists in the narrative tension between the representation of reality (*mimesis*) and poetic creation (*poiesis*). The novelist both reveals historical antagonisms and anticipates utopian resolutions to those problems (11-13).

In an unusual move, Schrader bypasses the discussion of other eighteenth- or nineteenth-century novels to concentrate on Robert Musil's *Der Mann ohne Eigenschaften* [The Man Without Qualities] (1930) in the second half of her study. Musil's gigantic fragment develops a portrait of pre-World War I Austrian society centered on the figure of Ulrich, a privileged young member of the upper middle class who lacks a sense of purpose and direction. He adopts a critically distant attitude toward both himself and society, which serve as the objects of intellectual experiments conducted in the form of philosophical essays. As Schrader argues, the gap between individual subjectivity and modern technology has become so extreme in the twentieth century that one can no longer make a nostalgic appeal to outmoded organic concepts of the self. Musil introduces instead the concept of *Eigenschaftslosigkeit* [literally, the state of having no qualities or characteristics]. *Bildung* becomes a means of transforming and renewing our perception of reality through a form of hypothetical narration. In Musil's words, *Der Mann ohne Eigenschaften* is no longer a "Bildungsroman einer Person," but the "Bildungsroman einer Idee" (175). At this point we are clearly on the periphery of traditional concepts of the genre. Schrader makes suggestive comments on the role of narrative self-consciousness in the Bildungsroman but limits her contribution to the criticism of genre by offering a dauntingly complex analysis of only two oddly paired novels.

Heinz Schlaffer locates the potential critique of *Bildung* within the Bildungsroman itself in his 1978 essay "Exoterik und Esoterik in Goethes Romanen." Schlaffer writes during the heyday of reception theory in Germany but is strongly opposed to the notion that it is up to the reader to determine the meaning of the work (226). Schlaffer insists that Goethe's novels contain an "esoteric" subtext that counters the conservative values they affirm on the surface:

> Exoterisch bestätigen Goethes Romane die jeweils zeitgenössischen Ideen: Freiheit, Bildung, Sittlichkeit, Fortschritt; esoterisch enthüllen sie, wie im Komplex der Zeit diesen zur Ideologie entstellten Ideen die Negation innewohnt: Illusion, Entleerung, Naturverfallenheit, Tod (225).

[Exoterically Goethe's novels endorse their contemporary ideas: freedom, *Bildung*, morality, progress. Esoterically they reveal the inherent negativity of these ideas when they are distorted into ideology in the course of time: illusion, emptiness, degeneration, death.]

Reversing critical tradition, Schlaffer argues that Goethe's classical Bildungs-roman could just as well be labeled a "novel of destruction," a *Zerstörungsro-man* (222). Like Karl Schlechta (whom he cites approvingly), Schlaffer reserves particular venom for the members of the Tower Society, who prac-tice a brutal form of pedagogy that leaves corpses in its wake (219). There is an important difference between Schlaffer's reading of the novel and Schlechta's, however. Schlechta restricts himself to an intrinsic analysis, whereas Schlaffer identifies the source of the novel's esoteric negativity in the historical negativity of the bourgeois society in which it was written (225-26).

Schlaffer reads literary texts with an eye toward dissonance rather than harmony and then attributes this dissonance to unresolved historical problems. Hence Schlaffer refers to his interpretations as "socio-historical resolutions of literary contradictions" (1973). In an earlier study of Jean Paul's *Titan* Schlaffer points out that the protagonist frequently dreams of heroic action, but never carries out his plans. Albano remains a non-hero in a world that no longer needs heroics. In his view, both *Titan* and Hölderlin's *Hyperion* reflect the failure of the revolution to solve the problems of the middle class. To blame, however, is ultimately the economic structure of capitalist society. The Bildungsroman blunders into a dilemma by opposing unified individuals to a reality based on the division of labor and by responding to a bourgeois econo-my with an aristocratic life style (45). Here Schlaffer writes like a traditional Marxist; more innovative is his linkage of formal breaks in the texts to socio-historical problems, an approach that reveals the influence of both Ludwig Marcuse and Theodor Adorno. Jean Paul's great achievement lies in his refusal to harmonize aesthetically a problem that in reality is unresolvable. "Im Mißlingen, im halben Gelingen bringt sich die Macht der realen Verhältnisse zur Geltung — genau an dem Punkt, an dem das Kunstwerk diese Macht zu mildern, in Form zu verwandeln trachtet" [The force of real circumstances asserts itself in failure, in half-success—precisely at that point where the work of art tries to soften this force, to convert it into form] (148).

The officially sanctioned poetics of the Bildungsroman in the former German Democratic Republic seem quite conservative in comparison with Western *Ideologiekritik*. While Heinz Schlaffer teased the esoteric critique out of seemingly affirmative texts, the socialist writer was to portray the develop-ment of the hero from a set a negative values — either fascism or just anti-social individualism — to his or her "arrival" in socialism (Trommler 1971, 155). The hero of this "literature of arrival" (*Ankunftsliteratur*) progresses from error to insight and from alienation to integration in his struggle for the socialist cause. Here we encounter a phenomenon that will recur in several feminist arguments of the 1980s as committed critics enlist a conservative understanding of the Bildungsroman — one that coincides neatly with definitions of the genre published in reference works of the 1950s (Wilpert 1955, Borcherdt 1958) — for use in a progressive cause. As Frank Trommler observes in his survey of the "Entwicklungsroman in der DDR" (1971), however, several of the most prominent examples of the genre published during the 1950s and 1960s prove less optimistic and more socially critical in practice than the theory would have us believe.

Perhaps inevitably, the search for irony and negativity in the German Bildungsroman during the 1970s soon provoked reassertions of a more traditional understanding of the genre. For example, Albert Berger borrows categories from Schiller's aesthetics to characterize Wilhelm Meister's development in what he terms Goethe's prototypical Bildungsroman (1977). Meister begins the novel directly engaged in the world of art. While he eventually abandons the theater, Meister gradually learns to view the world aesthetically. In Natalie he meets a true *schöne Seele*, the embodiment of Schiller's aesthetic form, and Wilhelm Meister himself enters Schiller's "aesthetic condition" in the novel's happy ending.

At first glance it might seem that the direct application of Schiller's aesthetic categories to Goethe's text imposes an overly abstract and overly optimistic grid onto what Schlaffer terms a *Zerstörungsroman*. Berger avoids the charge of naive optimism by adopting the same strategy employed by Lawrence Ryan and Gerda Röder in their interpretations of *Hyperion* and the *Lehrjahre:* when one learns to view the world aesthetically, one realizes that suffering and death are part of the whole. Thus, Berger argues that we must recognize the depths of Wilhelm's despair near the end of the novel: in the hours before the sudden turn for the best Wilhelm is "a deeply tragic figure" (167). Having brought his hero to hopeless despair, Goethe then supplies a moment of aesthetic transcendence. To be sure, Berger concludes, such an aesthetic ideal remains distant from Goethe's historical reality; yet the work of art offers signs of hope to those "who refuse to be satisfied with what happens to be the case" (176).

The Norwegian critic Ivar Sagmo makes a similar attempt to reemphasize the affirmative interpretation of the Bildungsroman in an increasingly skeptical critical climate (1982). Sagmo focuses primarily on Wilhelm Meister's "cognitive-psychic development" in Goethe's "most optimistic work" (237), the *Lehrjahre*. Wilhelm must learn to "see" the world around him in a particular Goethean sense; that is, he has to give up his subjective understanding of reality to obtain insight into the objective state of affairs in the world (69). His path leads him through the theater and also through an ascending series of female figures culminating in Natalie, who embodies "Freiheit in der Erscheinung" [freedom in appearance] (55). With less subtlety than Berger, Sagmo imposes Schiller's theoretical terminology onto the novel without regard for Goethe's ironic "tick." Sagmo maintains further that Meister's personal development contains historico-philosophical implications. Wilhelm must abandon his anachronistic belief in a poetically heroic form of existence and his equally anachronistic belief in tragic fate. He must learn to take matters into his own hands in accordance with Goethe's belief in the human freedom to shape the world: "die Zukunft [wird] zum sittlichen Auftrag der Menschheit" [the future {becomes} a moral mandate of humanity] (235). At this point Sagmo reduces Goethe's subtly ironic novel to an Enlightenment tract that preaches the virtues of self-reliance.

The German Bildungsroman in the English-Speaking World

Some of the most significant postwar contributions to the study of the German Bildungsroman came from Britain and the United States. From their vantage point outside Germany critics explored the connections between German history, the concept of *Bildung*, and the Bildungsroman. In his *The German Novel* (1956) Roy Pascal sets out to introduce English-speaking readers to the neglected tradition of the German novel. He views the Bildungsroman as "the novel-form in which the deepest spiritual issues of modern German society could take tangible shape" (98). The first third of the book is devoted to the analysis of four prominent examples of the genre: Goethe's *Wilhelm Meister*, Keller's *Der grüne Heinrich*, Stifter's *Nachsommer*, and Mann's *Der Zauberberg*. Pascal adds nothing new to the definition of the Bildungsroman, which he views as "the story of the formation of a character up to the moment when he ceases to be self-centred and becomes society-centred, thus beginning to shape his true self" (11). Pascal does have a good eye, however, for "how difficult was the way and how precarious the attainment" of *Bildung* in these novels (299). For example, he points out that Stifter can only write a successful Bildungsroman by deliberately excluding all troubling aspects of his contemporary society from the novel, and that Hans Castorp finds no practical use in the flatlands for what he has learned on the magic mountain.

Pascal surveys the work of five major German novelists in the remainder of his book. In addition to Franz Kafka and Thomas Mann, who were already familiar to an international audience, he chooses Jeremias Gotthelf, Wilhelm Raabe, and Theodor Fontane. For the most part Pascal offers sensible comments on individual texts, although he never seeks to conceal what he considers the artistic shortcomings of particular authors. As he explains in his conclusion, he does not want to mislead the reader who might decide to read some of the novels he introduces. Pascal often formulates his objections aptly and with catchy turns of phrase. Thus, he characterizes Stifter as "a mild and timid liberal" (53) and concedes that the unsympathetic reader may find Gotthelf to be a "pig-headed, self-willed, rampageous backwoodsman" (141). Often, however, Pascal is needlessly dismissive of writers and their works. He does not hesitate to point out "the great weakness" of Goethe's novel (28), dismisses Novalis's *Heinrich von Ofterdingen* as an inferior work of art (31), finds portions of *Der grüne Heinrich* "tedious" (43), and declares that Jean Paul's novels are "immensely irritating" (31).

Two basic convictions underlie Pascal's querulous comments: that the major German contribution to the novel is the Bildungsroman, and that the Bildungsroman is an inherently dull genre. When the Germans try to write social novels their efforts are, he thinks, infinitely inferior to the achievements of the Russians, French, and English. In "even the best German novels" Pascal finds "a sad lack of the energy and bite of passion" (301). The novels suffer from a "paucity of incident," a "lack of vividness"; they are "provincial, philistine" (302-03). In short, "to read the great German novels is mostly a 'cultural task' — infinitely rewarding, I believe, but never likely to become a dangerous passion in the reader!" (304). At this point one can only admire Pascal's fortitude in undertaking what seems to have been an arduous cultural task in the service of an inevitably ungrateful reader.

Jerome Hamilton Buckley utters similarly disapproving comments about the German Bildungsroman in the introduction to his volume on English examples of the genre (1974). Buckley views the Bildungsroman as a genre about growing up: the young male hero goes through a development that usually contains certain "principal elements — childhood, the conflict of generations, provinciality, the larger society, self-education, alienation, ordeal by love, the search for a vocation and a working philosophy" (18). In adopting the German term Buckley blithely disregards questions that have been central to the genre, including its "essential" Germanness, its implication in nineteenth-century ideology, and its relation to German theories of *Bildung*. Moreover, Buckley shows little respect or understanding for what he terms "the prototype of the form" (vii), *Wilhelm Meisters Lehrjahre*. Like Pascal, Buckley is unable to resist giving a few swift kicks to the character Goethe once referred to as a "poor dog" before moving on to the study of the (vastly superior) English novel. As Jeffrey Sammons observes,

> one is not obliged to admire *Wilhelm Meister*, but to deny oneself access to it by measuring it against evaluative canons with which it has nothing to do and then appropriate the literary-historical term largely flowing from it seems more than a little arrogantly provincial. (1991, 36)

W. Witte offers an apologetic response to the charge that the German Bildungsroman is "alien corn" that is "not for export" (1979-80). He address-es two issues that have been raised in connection with the genre. The first involves the sociopolitical question whether self-cultivation precludes service to the community; the second is aesthetic, whether the attempt to portray "a man's development from childhood to maturity" is "apt to be heavy going" (90). Witte observes sensibly that the tendency toward intellectual abstraction and the portrayal of emotional experience rather than external event need not be "construed as a damning charge" (89). Citing Thomas Mann as a positive example, he also questions whether self-cultivation must necessarily be selfish. Witte concludes his brief defense of the Bildungsroman with an appreciation of Mann as the novelist best suited to bridge the gap between the German and European novel tradition.

W. H. Bruford probes more deeply into the political consequences of the German preoccupation with *Bildung* in his wide-ranging study *The German Tradition of Self-Cultivation* (1975). He seeks to answer the most troubling question confronting postwar studies of German society and culture: how could the people who had celebrated the works of Goethe and Schiller em-brace Hitler as their *Führer?* Bruford centers his study around the concept of *Bildung*, and although he considers important authors of the Bildungsroman from Goethe to Thomas Mann, he extends his analysis to the statesman Wilhelm von Humboldt, the theologian Friedrich Schleiermacher, the philoso-phers Arthur Schopenhauer and Friedrich Nietzsche, and the professor of aesthetics Friedrich Theodor Vischer.

Bruford begins by tracing the humanist concept of *Bildung* as it emerged in the works of Humboldt, Goethe, and Schleiermacher. Already in these writers he finds troubling limitations to primarily positive ideals. Citing Kurt May, Bruford stresses the restricted nature of Wilhelm Meister's attained *Bildung* in the *Lehrjahre* and points out that the utopia of the *Wanderjahre* is "strongly authoritarian and patriarchal" (103). He identifies the potential for disaster in Schleiermacher's belief in the historical uniqueness of every nation combined with his "Romantic irrationalism, the idea of self-dedication to an ideal, no matter what" (86). He even suggests that the aristocratic Humboldt's belief in relentless self-improvement serves as a strategy "to escape the boredom which always threatens an over-leisured class" (17).

Schopenhauer, Vischer, and Nietzsche restrict the concept of *Bildung* to an increasingly narrow elite. Bruford portrays Schopenhauer as a crotchety, somewhat eccentric bachelor who splits society into a handful of self-right-eous geniuses, on the one hand, and the inferior masses on the other. Schopenhauer combines his disdain for the mob with a belief in authoritarian government and open misogyny. If it were not for his sense of humor, Bruford continues, Vischer "would be an intolerable intellectual snob" who also found women inferior and democracy repulsive (163). The devolution of the humanist concept of *Bildung* reaches its nadir in Nietzsche, whose "idea of 'Bildung' was becoming rather a consciousness of what separated him, and intellectually superior people like him, from the general mass, and made them indispensable as leaders" (171). While other "decadent" European artists sought to shock the complacent bourgeoisie, it was only the Germans who used "living dangerously" to justify militaristic expansionism (189). Bruford concludes "that there are not two Germanies, a bad and a good, but only one, whose best gifts turned through some devil's art to evil" (263). Taken together, the apolitical inwardness of most Germans, the reduction of *Bildung* to a status symbol among the educated class, and the appropriation of the concept by self-appointed, ruthless leaders transformed an eighteenth-century ideal into an intolerant ideology of chauvinism, nationalism, and militarism.

R. Hinton Thomas supplements Bruford's inquiry into the inherent dangers in the German concept of *Bildung* by concentrating on the work of several late nineteenth-century historians and political theorists who transferred the concept of *Bildung* from the individual to the group. For example, Heinrich Treitschke views the "state as an organism, governed by its own inner laws of development, by virtue of which the German 'Volk' had a destiny all its own to be lived out" (1977, 180). Thus, "the training of 'personality'" is seen as "the means with which to achieve a strong 'Volkstum'" (182). While Thomas agrees with Bruford that the notion of personal *Bildung* becomes increasingly difficult in industrial society, he points out that collective self-cultivation of the *Volk* flourished. In the process, the emancipatory concept turns "to serve the interests of restriction and repression." Thus, *Bildung* not only "accepted a highly conservative social order, but ideologically fostered it" (184).

In 1974 David Miles addressed a broad English-speaking audience with his essay on "The Changing Image of the Hero in the German Bildungsroman." Miles bases his argument on two character types, "the 'picaro' (the nondeveloping hero, the unselfconscious adventurer or man of action) and the 'confessor' (the hero of personality growth, the introspective hero, the protagonist of consciousness, memory, and guilt)" (980). Although Miles could not have known it at the time, Mikhail Bakhtin had already explored this distinction in his typology of the novel form in the 1930s. Miles derives his typology from the opening chapter of Erich Auerbach's *Mimesis* (1946), where Auerbach contrasts the static figure of Homer's Odysseus with the developing characters of the Pentateuch.

Miles concentrates on three novels: the *Lehrjahre*, Keller's *Der grüne Heinrich*, and Rainer Maria Rilke's *Die Aufzeichnungen des Malte Laurids Brigge* [The Notebooks of Malte Laurids Brigge] (1910). Contrary to common opinion, he argues that Wilhelm Meister lacks character depth. Like the

picaro, this "strangely *un*psychological" figure shows little internal development in the course of the novel (981). Only the distanced, ironic narrator
represents the "clear, harmonious, serene personality" we would expect of an
"'educational hero'" (983-84). The sense of psychological development on the
part of the protagonist increases in *Der grüne Heinrich*, largely because
Heinrich Lee has become the narrator of his own *Bildung* (in the second
version of the novel). Like several previous authors, Miles transfers the site
of *Bildung* from current events to the recollection and narration of past experience: the picaro becomes a confessor. The process culminates in Rilke's
novel, where Malte retreats into the memory of his childhood and the act of
its narration.

In conclusion, Miles argues that the Bildungsroman should not be viewed
solely in terms of the increased interiority of the picaresque hero, as Thomas
Mann had suggested, but also as a "secularization of the confessional hero of
religious fiction" (990). Now, E. L. Stahl had already argued in 1934 that the
Bildungsroman should be understood as arising from the confluence of the
adventure novel and the religious autobiography in which each genre undergoes a transformation in the process of its merger. But Stahl's narrative leads
up to the *Lehrjahre*, whereas Miles uses Goethe's novel as a point of departure. Most critics trace the gradual demise of the genre in the wake of Goethe's prototypical work, but Miles sees the movement toward Rilke as a
positive development. Thus, he writes of "Heinrich's advance over Wilhelm
as an educational hero" (986). Here Miles exaggerates Meister's lack of
development, for the encounter with Werner toward the end of the novel
makes clear that Meister has at least progressed far beyond his friend. After
tracing a gradual increase in narrative introspection up to Rilke, Miles then
signals the end of the tradition. We are left only with Kafka's drastically
problematic world or the literary parodies of Mann and Grass.

Martin Swales's *The German Bildungsroman from Wieland to Hesse*
(1978a) is the most important contribution to the topic since Jürgen Jacobs's
Wilhelm Meister und seine Brüder (1972). We left Jacobs in the awkward
position of having written a substantial study of the German Bildungsroman
in which he finds it extremely difficult to find examples of the genre. Swales
tackles Jacobs's theory of an "unfulfilled genre" head-on in his introduction
pointing out an essential difference between biological and literary categories:
each new member of a biological species does not change the species as a
whole, whereas each work of literature adds something new to its genre.
Thus, one should not set out into the literary jungles armed with a rigid
understanding of genre that is almost certain to be outsmarted by particular
texts. Indeed, "only pulp literature fully interlocks with its genre expectation"
(11).

Swales appeals to the concept of the "hermeneutic circle" in his under-standing of genre (10). We come to a novel with certain expectations, and "the specific work activates and energizes those expectations in order to debate with them, to refashion, to challenge, perhaps even to parody them" (11). Central to Swales's argument, therefore, is that a Bildungsroman need not fulfill the expectations it arises to still be considered an example of the genre: "As long as the model of the genre is intimated as a sustained and sustaining presence in the work in question, then the genre retains its validity as a structuring principle within the palpable stuff of an individual literary creation" (12). In fact, it is the very refusal of the Bildungsroman to resolve all tension that makes for the high artistic quality of the genre. Thus, Swales identifies "the openness, the obliqueness of Goethe's novel" as "the deepest source of the book's meaning" (26). Major examples of the genre reveal a "pervasive tentativeness of the narrative undertaking," a "hedging of bets" (30), "consistently sustained irresolution" (35).

Swales demonstrates his thesis in intelligent readings of canonical texts by paying particular attention to ironic narration. He includes chapters on Wieland's *Agathon*, Goethe's *Wilhelm Meisters Lehrjahre*, Stifter's *Nachsommer*, Keller's *Der grüne Heinrich*, Mann's *Der Zauberberg*, and Hermann Hesse's *Das Glasperlenspiel* [The Glass Bead Game] (1943). For Swales, the very structure of the novels makes it impossible for the author to portray completely successful development. At any given moment an individual has many potential options, but as time goes on only a limited number of these experiences can be pursued. Swales identifies this tension between "linear time and practical activity, that is, between potentiality and actuality" as "central to the process of thematic argument of the Bildungsroman" (29). He uses this structural model to define the novels' relation to the "German tradition of self-cultivation." Noting that the German preoccupation with *Bildung* has been viewed "as a cornerstone of that quiescent, unpolitical bourgeois ideology which made German liberalism such a half-hearted phe-nomenon" (152), he holds that the very open-ended nature of the novels examined makes them "anything but unreflected didacticism; it is, rather, the supreme enactment of that problematic which [Leonard] Krieger and others so precisely perceive" (157), the German concept of freedom that combines "'secular submission and spiritual independence'" (155). In other words, the concept of *Bildung* may encourage compliance with existing authority, but the Bildungsroman remains free to question the implications of this decision. As Swales put it in a lecture the same year his book was published, "if we want to look for a critique of *Bildung*, the Bildungsroman is an obvious and elo-quent starting point" (1978b, 62-63).

Michael Beddow stresses the emancipatory potential of plausible fictions in his study of the Bildungsroman (1982). His work typifies the turn toward a qualified reaffirmation of humanistic values we have seen in Berger and Sagmo. Beddow is well aware that his approach may seem unfashionable, yet he cautions against the danger of imposing late-twentieth-century skepticism onto "the art of earlier times" (73). The authors of the Bildungsroman do insert ironic qualifications concerning the nature of *Bildung* into their works, but we should not throw out the baby with the bath in the rush to rob the texts of their utopian power.

Beddow develops extensive readings of five of the same novels examined by Martin Swales, omitting Hesse's *Das Glasperlenspiel*. He contends that it is not the development of the hero that is the central concern of the Bildungsroman; instead, it is the self-conscious fictionality of the works. He maintains that it is precisely our awareness of the fictional status of the texts that "offers insights into human nature which could not be adequately conveyed either in the form of discursive arguments or through a rigorously mimetic, non-self-conscious fictional work" (5). For example, Wieland gives *Agathon* the semblance of greater truth by undermining the expectations of conventional fiction. Thus, the narrator deliberately distances himself from the novel's implausibly happy ending. Yet the irony is not comprehensive; the rejection of fictional stereotypes "is the major device by which the novel attempts to persuade us of the essential truth of what it represents" (59). Goethe also highlights the fictionality of his novel's conclusion, but not to refute the process of *Bildung* it portrays. "Self-clarification and self-expression" can only be brought to "such a triumphant completion" in an overtly fictional work, but the process itself remains "a fundamental feature of all authentically human experience" even if it does not reach completion in reality (139-40).

Beddow goes on to examine the relation between fiction and reality in Stifter's *Nachsommer* and Keller's *Der grüne Heinrich*. Despite important differences between the two novelists, both are said to invert the patterns of their eighteenth-century predecessors in that they "cast severe doubt upon the worth of any sense of self which is not derived from respect for an external order" (160). Perception and acceptance of given reality takes precedence over "the claims of unaccommodated imagination" (160); "self-effacing receptiveness" replaces "self-realization" (188). Thomas Mann restores the liberating power of self-conscious fiction to the Bildungsroman in *Der Zauberberg*. Whereas previous critics had complained that in Castorp's dream Thomas Mann had sunk to the level of a crude allegory, Beddow praises the same vision because it "portrays fictive activity as a deeply rooted, spontaneous process within the self, and as a process with enormous power to affect reality" (268). Taken together, these nonmimetic Bildungsromane share

a belief that fictional constructions give access to truths beyond themselves, a conviction that imaginative creation is not merely a game

a belief that fictional constructions give access to truths beyond themselves, a conviction that imaginative creation is not merely a game
played according to its own particular rules, but also a mode of seeing
and revealing what the world beyond fiction is like. (286)

While readers may appreciate the subtlety of Beddow's individual interpretations and applaud his attempt to restore humanistic values to the Bildungsroman, his approach is nevertheless open to criticism. Readers in
today's skeptical intellectual climate may well question his confident ability
to identify the features of "authentically human experience" and may resist
his implication that we are morally flawed if we do not accept his point of
view. "If Goethe's distinctive humanism, as it is expressed in the *Lehrjahre*,
strikes us as naive or even untruthful," warns Beddow, "we had perhaps
better look to our own notions of human dignity and fulfillment before pre-
suming to cast the first stone" (158). Beddow elevates himself to a high moral
ground from which he looks disparagingly on those who would reduce literature to mere "textures of 'narrativity'" (286). This attitude lends an unpleas-
antly self-righteous tone to an otherwise solid study. The Bildungsroman has,
for Beddow, become a bulwark of traditional values in territory increasingly
infiltrated by contemporary literary theory.

4: New Directions in Bildungsroman Criticism

Social History and the Bildungsroman

Rolf-Peter Janz's article on the Bildungsroman in Horst Glaser's social history of German literature (1980) reveals the extent to which the general understanding of the genre had changed since the immediate postwar years. Whereas earlier critics had viewed the Bildungsroman as the socially affirmative record of successful personal maturation, Janz stresses the difficulties confronting personal *Bildung* in historical context. In brief overviews of classical and romantic novels from the *Lehrjahre* to Eichendorff's *Ahnung und Gegenwart*, he observes that novelists either project harmony onto a distant age or demonstrate the difficulty the middle-class protagonist has in finding meaningful activity in a world still ruled by the aristocracy. Janz concludes that the novels that create the tradition of the Bildungsroman between 1795 and 1815 demonstrate that they are not Bildungsromane at all — at least not if one defines the genre in terms of the intended reconciliation of the individual with empirical reality (162).

Rolf Selbmann provides a more detailed analysis of the social history of the German novel by concentrating on the function of the theater in the eighteenth- and nineteenth-century Bildungsroman (1981). During the eighteenth century such writers as Lessing, Schiller, and Goethe sought to establish a national theater in Germany that would educate the middle class, criticize the existing social structure, and encourage reform. Not surprisingly, therefore, both Moritz's Anton Reiser and the Wilhelm Meister of the *Sendung* turn to the theater when they first leave home. For Anton Reiser, however, the theater functions more as an escape into a fantasy world than as a medium for social reform. In the *Lehrjahre* life in the theater is no longer Wilhelm's ultimate goal, but it does serve as a necessary stage in his *Bildung*. Jean Paul soon rejects the classical notion of aesthetic education through the theater in the figure of Roquairol, who commits suicide on stage in *Titan*, and by the middle of the nineteenth century writers had abandoned the dream of a progressive national theater altogether. Thus, Selbmann refutes the common assumption that the German Bildungsroman focuses solely on the private sphere and is therefore incompatible with the social novel. In his view the Bildungsroman *is* a social novel, and the nexus of the private and the public in the novel is the theater.

Like many critics before him, Selbmann displays a certain discomfort with the term *Bildungsroman*, and often substitutes the more neutral concept *Bildungsgeschichte* [story about *Bildung*] when discussing particular novels. Jeffrey Sammons goes further in his "The Mystery of the Missing *Bildungsroman*" when he concludes that he was pursuing a "phantom genre" (1981, 239). Sammons tells the tale of his futile quest with a welcome sense of humor, as one nineteenth-century German novel after the next fails to fit the pattern established by *Wilhelm Meisters Lehrjahre*. He does not question the existence of the genre itself, however, which he locates around 1800 and again in certain novels of the early twentieth century. Sammons argues that the process of canon formation falsified the facts of nineteenth-century literary history. If we look beyond the handful of canonical German novels of the nineteenth century we discover "historical, social, and political novels as well as individual novels; we find realistic novels both on large canvases and with strong regional focus" (238). Sammons maintains that the German novel was closer to the European social novel during this period than is generally recognized; canonical selectivity has obscured the facts of literary history. Moreover, "those books that now have canonical standing were obscure and were read, if at all, only by a thinly populated intellectual elite" (239).

While Sammons called attention to forgotten works of nineteenth-century German fiction, others highlighted the social content of canonical texts. For example, Gert Sautermeister focuses on the interrelation between individual subjectivity and objective social conditions in Keller's *Der grüne Heinrich*. He places particular stress on the function of Heinrich's father as the representative of a threefold enlightenment ideal: he is at once a diligent worker (*Wirtschaftsbürger*), a politically engaged public citizen, and a private aesthete (*Kulturbürger*) (1980: 84). He manages both to improve himself and to work for the betterment of society. In his ability to synthesize work, politics, and recreation he embodies the humanitarian ideal of the German Enlightenment and Classicism (85). Yet this combination could only occur during a brief historical period; the father's early death signals the precarious status of the ideal he represents. As Heinrich matures, it becomes increasingly evident that the changing economic structure of society works to undermine humanistic idealism. The gap between the classical tradition and contemporary reality becomes painfully evident during the communal performance of *Wilhelm Tell* depicted at some length midway through the novel. While the amateur actors proclaim the values of self-sacrifice for the common good in the performance, offstage they defend their own economic interests ruthlessly (105). Freedom, equality, and fraternity disappear under the pressures of private ownership and capitalist competition (106). Yet Heinrich fails to realize that his personal problems stem from changing social and economic conditions. Under the tyrannical influence of the paternal superego Heinrich blames himself and not the world around him for his difficulties. When near starvation in Munich the guilt-ridden son refuses to write to his mother until he attains financial success as a painter, but his failure is the result of market pressure external to himself. Heinrich's dilemma reveals a new stage in the history of the Bildungsroman as social wrongs become the source of self-accusation (114). In Sautermeister's view, Keller reveals the self-destructive effect of Heinrich's guilt most clearly in the first version of his novel. The revised novel offers a toned-down, compromised portrayal of the conflict that brings Keller's work closer to the classical Bildungsroman but thereby obscures the dilemma revealed so remorselessly in the first version (117-120).

Uwe-K. Ketelsen's analysis of Stifter's *Nachsommer* reflects a similar concern with the relation of the novel to its socio-historical context (1980). Like many previous critics, Ketelsen underscores the influence of the 1848 revolution on Stifter's work. He views Stifter's return to the aesthetics of German Classicism as a reaction against this eruption of chthonic passions. Ketelsen pays particular attention to the role of labor in Stifter's novel. Accumulated capital circulates silently behind the scenes and finances the efforts of the privileged class to construct an artificial paradise on their country estate. The carefully crafted form of the novel hardly reveals a heightened reality behind transient appearances. In Ketelsen's view, Stifter's *Nachsommer* seeks to annihilate historical reality through the aestheticization of everyday life (199).

Martin Swales addresses the relation between utopia and the Bildungsroman in his contribution to Wilhelm Voßkamp's anthology *Utopieforschung* [Utopia Research] (1982). Swales again stresses the unresolved tension between simultaneity and succession in the Bildungsroman, between the protagonist's seemingly unlimited potential and the inevitable sacrifices demanded by reality. He then uses this structural model to distinguish between the Bildungsroman and literary utopias. In both cases the utopia stands in opposition to reality. A utopian novel such as Johann Gottfried Schnabel's *Insel Felsenburg,* however, depicts an idealized community carefully isolated from the historical present, whereas in the Bildungsroman the tension between utopian projections and realistic surroundings takes place within the novel itself. The resulting texts present an ironic mixture of utopian sentiments and the psychological and social context of concrete experience (225).

In his own contribution to the same anthology Voßkamp examines "Utopie und Utopiekritik" [Utopia and Utopia Critique] in the *Lehrjahre* and the *Wanderjahre* (1982). Voßkamp identifies two separate utopian strains in the *Lehrjahre*: a *Bildungsutopie* of optimal personal development and a *Sozialutopie* represented by the Tower Society. Seen from a European perspective the enlightened absolutism of the Tower Society seems reactionary, but within the context of German society it contains progressive, utopian moments. The

individual and social utopias are related to one another, but the tension between them is not resolved. Rather, each relativizes the other, illustrating the
antagonism between the natural rights of the subject and the social necessity
of institutions. Goethe later renounces the utopia of many-sided *Bildung* for
the individual in favor of a social utopia for all in the *Wanderjahre* (237).
Goethe qualifies his new ideal, however, in the figure of Odoardo, whose
dictatorial powers transform the social model into the ironic citation of a
dystopia that serves as a critique of the utopian model (241). Thus both
Swales and Voßkamp reject the notion that the Bildungsroman portrays an
untroubled utopia; rather, the novels become battlegrounds where the struggle
between utopian hope and ironic realism takes place.

In an earlier article on the notion of genres as socio-literary institutions
(1977), Voßkamp had suggested that the emergence of the Bildungsroman was
closely tied to early attempts to distinguish between serious and popular
fiction during a period of explosive growth in literary production. One popular counterpart to the emerging Bildungsroman was what Helmut Germer
terms the "German novel of education" (1982). Germer compiles a useful
bibliography of these pedagogical treatises in fictional form and provides
information about their authors, publishers, and readers in eighteenth-century
Germany. His work reminds us of how few of the novels written during this
period made their way into the literary canon. Moreover, his description of
these narrowly didactic works highlights the aesthetic complexity and the
social criticism of the Bildungsroman itself.

Klaus-Dieter Sorg reveals just this complexity by stressing the lack of
narrative closure in the German Bildungsroman (1983). Sorg understands the
Bildungsroman as a literary answer to the collapse of what once seemed
adequate ways of understanding the world (7). Whereas novelists of the mid
eighteenth century had sought to guide the reader to a set of predetermined
virtues, the new process of *Bildung* remained open-ended. Authors of the
Bildungsroman attempted to impose a unifying order on events even as they
unfolded toward an uncertain future. The process is by its nature inconclusive. Sorg argues that the Bildungsroman *cannot* come to a convincing conclusion: it is an open discourse in response to a problem for which there is no
suitable solution (8). Problems can be resolved only at the cost of ideology
(46), a fact Hegel had already recognized, but later critics forgot.

Sorg examines four novels in clearly written and intelligently argued
chapters. He claims that *Wilhelm Meisters Lehrjahre* is a Bildungsroman
because it is not based on the relationship between a mentor and his pupil.
Wilhelm searches for his own peculiar form of life, but this search remains
inconclusive; there is no convincing solution of all problems in the text (79).
Similarly, Sorg views Stifter's *Nachsommer* as a Bildungsroman *not* because
of the harmonious development it portrays, but rather because it reveals the

violent suppression of discord necessary to attain this harmony. Heinrich Lee finds it impossible to perceive his life meaningfully. Instead, *Der grüne Heinrich* reveals a great gap between Heinrich's social status at the end of the novel and his insight into the meaninglessness of the most important aspects of reality (159). Finally, Sorg argues that Thomas Mann oversimplifies his own novel in seeking to impose his democratic ideals onto *Der Zauberberg;* Castorp's uncertain development after the "Schnee" chapter reveals difficulties in Mann's own beliefs.

Michael Minden counters what he identifies as a trend toward structural analysis in "The Place of Inheritance in the Bildungsroman" (1983). Focusing primarily on Stifter's *Nachsommer*, Minden notes that the "circularity of inheritance ... counterbalances the linearity of progression which we are more accustomed to discern" in the Bildungsroman (256). In Stifter's paean to bourgeois values the hero inherits his place in the world rather than achieving it through his own efforts, "and the book's denouement, its fulfillment, and a main element in its climax is the *size* of the marriage settlement" (259). While Wieland and Goethe leave tensions unresolved in the conclusions of their novels, Stifter cannot tolerate uncertainty. The extreme nature of Stifter's work enables us to perceive most clearly how the notion of art implied in the genre of the Bildungsroman is characterized by an ordering through the control and regulation worked by its representations. It promotes authority in the very activity of representation. (288) In Minden's view, Kafka's work evokes "the claustrophobic sense of imprisonment which is the logical other side to Stifter's attempts to close all the doors and bar all the windows" (291).

Helga Esselborn-Krumbiegel (1983) returns to the study of the *Entwicklungsroman* in the early twentieth century that had been the subject of Charlotte Kehr's ideologically tainted 1939 dissertation. Whereas Kehr traced the genre to a moment of triumphant nationalism in which the individual was subordinated to the state, Esselborn-Krumbiegel develops a typology of novels that reveal the disintegration of the modern subject. She constructs an ideally typical structural model of the genre that serves as the standard against which she measures its subsequent deviations. In the "epigonal *Entwicklungsroman*" characters from the lower classes achieve financial security and higher social status by dint of virtues they possess from the outset; other novels continue the tradition of the Romantic *Künstlerroman* by depicting self-absorbed individuals who remain excluded from the rest of society. The most extreme transformation of the genre occurs in the *Subjektroman*, as exemplified by Hesse's *Demian* (1919), Rilke's *Malte*, and Robert Musil's *Die Verwirrungen des Zöglings Törleß* [The Confusions of Young Törless] (1906). In these works the hero appears only negatively at first, as a gap [*Leerstelle*], as the point of intersection of oscillating forces, as an empty form (137). The subject then constructs itself, not in opposition to a hostile environment but by assimilating elements of the reality it experiences (138). Beyond the *Subjektroman* lie three types of novels allegedly so different from the *Entwicklungsroman* as to constitute separate genres: the *Zeitroman*, more concerned with portraying a particular epoch than an individual; the *Demonstrationsroman*, where the hero serves to express a preformed idea (for example, Hesse's *Siddhartha*); and finally the parody of the *Entwicklungsroman* such as one finds in the novels of Thomas Mann.

As with any attempt at a classification, Esselborn-Krumbiegel runs the risk of oversimplifying particular texts in the effort to assign them a place in her system. Taxonomic zeal becomes more extreme in Randolph P. Shaffner's *The Apprenticeship Novel* (1984). After sensibly stressing "the purely regulative value of common-denominator classifications" (7), Shaffner provides "an itemized checklist of several distinguishing traits" of the apprenticeship novel (17) and then compiles a detailed list of German, English, and French novels that have been associated with the genre. He adopts the term *apprenticeship novel* as a convenient translation of the genre's prototype, Goethe's *Lehrjahre*. Shaffner identifies three stages in the apprenticeship of the hero: an initial release from the bondage of self-delusion, reintegration into the community, and reflections on the metaphysical problem of death. Here again the interpretive grid takes precedence over the novels themselves, for no single work combines all three phases: Shaffner places the first five books of the *Lehrjahre* together with Somerset Maugham's *Of Human Bondage* (1915) in stage one, the rest of the *Lehrjahre* in stage two, and *Der Zauberberg* in stage three.

Hartmut Steinecke presents the results of his earlier study of German novel theory in streamlined form in his essay "*Wilhelm Meister* und die Folgen" ['Wilhelm Meister' and the Consequences] (1984). We recall that Jeffrey Sammons had noted how few German novels of the later nineteenth century conformed to the model of the Bildungsroman. Steinecke agrees that it is indeed difficult to find a successful nineteenth-century Bildungsroman. His primary interest, however, lies less in the study of particular texts than in the way in which Goethe's *Lehrjahre* and *Wanderjahre* shaped nineteenth-century theories of the novel. Conservative critics embraced Goethe's novels and their politics while radical critics either rejected their inwardness or reinterpreted them into social novels, but no one ignored them. It was only when Wilhelminian critics accepted Dilthey's conservative definition of the Bildungsroman that the discussion of the genre constricted to the study of a special sort of novel to which were attributed "typically German" characteristics in a naively patriotic way. Thus, Steinecke proposes that we replace *Bildungsroman* with *Individualroman*. This new term could encompass the complexity of novels written in the tradition of the *Lehrjahre* in the period before Dilthey, without being burdened by its association with conservative ideology. As in the case of other recent attempts to rename the genre, however, there is as yet no evidence that the scholarly community is willing to accept Steinecke's suggestion (see also Steinecke 1987, 53-75; trans. in Hardin 1991, 69-96).

The same might be said for Hartmut Laufhütte's proposed term *Biographie-Erzählung* (1984, 38). In a sharp response to recent studies of *Der grüne Heinrich* he contends that Keller's novel is not a Bildungsroman and that we should restrict use of the term to a few works written around 1800. Dissatisfaction with the term *Bildungsroman* becomes even more extreme in Frederick Amrine's critical reassessment of the genre (1987). His survey of previous criticism reveals a confusing picture, as opinion regarding what constitutes a Bildungsroman has fluctuated between complete skepticism and vague generosity:

> And there we have the problem: if one takes "Bildung" in its strict and limited historical sense, then nothing is a *Bildungsroman* — not even *Wilhelm Meisters Lehrjahre*; but if one takes it in the loose sense, something like "development of the protagonist," then *everything* is a *Bildungsroman*. (127)

Amrine concludes that the Bildungsroman represents such an "extreme of imprecision" when compared to other genres that we should "recognize the term for what it is: a place-holder at best" (136). He suggests that we dispense "with the 'phlogiston' of *Bildung*" when studying novels associated with the genre and view them instead as "*generic hybrids*" containing elements "of the picaresque novel, the *Trivialroman*, the Gothic novel, and the romance" (134). I would argue that continued use of the term *Bildungsroman* does not preclude investigation into the genre's ties to other literary traditions. Moreover, the genre has entered into the vocabulary of literary terms, and justified attention to its notorious imprecision is unlikely to make it go away.

While critics of German literature were busy questioning the validity of the Bildungsroman and thinning out its ranks to at best a handful of texts, Franco Moretti incorporated the history of the nineteenth-century European novel into his comparative study of the Bildungsroman (1987). Moretti argues that the Bildungsroman arises in response to the disorienting historical changes in Europe at the end of eighteenth century. Youth acquired new significance during this period as individuals could no longer expect to mature into the stable world of their parents. Moretti argues that the evolving protagonists of the new Bildungsroman do more than reflect the uncertainties of the age; they also help to shape an understanding of the events that produced them and to which they respond:

Europe plunges into modernity, but without possessing a *culture* of
modernity. If youth, therefore, achieves its symbolic centrality, and
the "great narrative" of the *Bildungsroman* comes into being, this is
because Europe has to attach a meaning, not so much to youth, as to
modernity. (5)

In viewing the Bildungsroman as the "'symbolic form' of modernity" (5)
Moretti aligns himself with Hegel, Lukács, and Bakhtin. As a "historian of
culture" (213) he traces the links between literary form and the transformation
of society under the pressures of modernism. He moves easily among literary
texts; nineteenth-century thinkers including Marx, Darwin, and Nietzsche;
and contemporary literary theory without crushing the reader under the weight
of his erudition.

Like most critics, Moretti locates the origin of the Bildungsroman in
Wilhelm Meisters Lehrjahre. He views the *Lehrjahre* as Goethe's response to
the French Revolution, in which he envisions the possibility of personal
happiness in a stable society. As Moretti points out, however, Goethe's novel
has the quality of a fairy tale that excludes social problems from its utopian
solution. Moreover, the members of the Tower Society impose their will on
the reluctant hero: "Wilhelm *is forced to be happy* in spite of his intentions"
(21).

Moretti then follows the Bildungsroman to France. For Stendhal, the
cultivation of the self stands in opposition to public behavior, and the novel
must have an unhappy ending. Balzac reverses the problem, as his heroes
display neither depth of character nor the desire to change the world. They
accept society as it is and seek only to adapt themselves for social success
better than their rivals. The Bildungsroman ends in Flaubert's cynical world,
where "maturity appears to be — nothing. A void, an empty hole between a
somewhat vile youth and an imbecilic old age" (179).

With the exception of Jane Austen and George Eliot, the English novelists
do not address the problem of youth in a changing world that preoccupies the
authors of the Continental Bildungsroman. The English had had their revolution in the seventeenth century, and English society remained comparatively
stable during the next two centuries. Thus the protagonist of the British novel

is certainly not expected to establish a moral universe that already
exists, eternal and unchangeable, and even less to question that universe. His most typical function lies rather in making that world
recognizable for any and all readers. (189)

Personal development confirms innate qualities rather than creating new
potential. Moretti argues that this "devaluation of youth" to "a haphazard and

dangerous interlude" reflects the values of a democratic society (204). The English Bildungsroman is a juridical fairy tale that propagates the liberal-democratic desire for universal law.

Like Lukács, Moretti paints in broad strokes, basing his history of the nineteenth-century European novel on a relatively small number of acknowl-edged classics. Germanists might object that his reading of the *Lehrjahre* covers much familiar territory, and that he ignores other German novelists entirely. Yet the scope and suggestiveness of Moretti's undertaking more than compensate for these shortcomings. Of particular interest is his understanding of the relation between Goethe's *Lehrjahre* and the European novel. In Moretti's view, this prototypical German Bildungsroman becomes not the exception to the European novel, but its most representative form.

In my own recent book (1992) I view the Bildungsroman in the context of the changing literary institution in Germany around 1800. These changes involved the rapid expansion of literary production, the growth of a middle-class readership, and the beginnings of artistic professionalism. The new literature played an important role in what Jürgen Habermas has termed the public sphere as a forum for the dissemination and development of ideas. Although the absolutist governments of politically fragmented Germany excluded most citizens from participation in state affairs, the public sphere served as a prepolitical arena that could build consensus and at least create the potential for reform. Thus, literature served as a point of intersection between the individual and society as the public medium molded the development of private lives.

Not surprisingly, then, the protagonists of the Bildungsromane of the period are avid readers, and most take part in some form of artistic produc-tion as well. The common motif of the reading hero suggests that individual development proceeds through the assimilation of literary models; examples range from Anton Reiser's unconscious citation of *Werther* to Kater Murr's plagiarism of Shakespeare. From this perspective, the self is not an organic whole but a fictional construct. By making their protagonists artists, more-over, the novelists address their own relations with the public. The works of such professional writers as Ludwig Tieck, Jean Paul, and E. T. A. Hoffmann suggest that despite theories of aesthetic autonomy and the Roman-tics' insistence on the utter incompatibility between artistic production and financial concerns, authors were bound to society in an uneasy alliance ob-scured by idealistic rhetoric. By the time Hoffmann was writing in the reac-tionary climate of postrevolutionary Berlin, it was clear that the utopian dreams of the Weimar Classicists and the early Romantics were not to be realized. At the same time, the Bildungsroman incorporates a skeptical com-mentary on the process of *Bildung* even in its most idealistic period, and that skepticism remains an integral part of the genre throughout the nineteenth and twentieth centuries.

In short, I view the Bildungsroman as a literary genre that examines the changing function of fiction in German culture, both in the shaping of individual consciousness and as the medium for the aesthetic education of society. In addition to the Habermasian notion of the public sphere I draw on both Mikhail Bakhtin's concept of "heteroglossia" in the novel and Stephan Greenblatt's study of Renaissance "self-fashioning." Perhaps most important, I argue against both mimetic concepts of art and the belief that art inhabits an autonomous realm. "Literature in this view neither repeats reality nor does it escape reality; instead, it *transforms* reality, and the *Bildungsroman* is the genre that examines this transformation" (11).

Taking Stock Again: Recent Bildungsroman Surveys

Publications by Lothar Köhn (1969) and Jürgen Jacobs (1972) marked a first attempt to gain an overview of the Bildungsroman and its criticism. The tempo of scholarly production soon increased sharply, and the mid 1980s scholars renewed their efforts to sort through the material that had accumulated in the meantime. Thus, Rolf Selbmann's *Der deutsche Bildungsroman* (1984) is primarily meant to be less an innovative addition to the field than an annotated bibliography of pertinent research materials. As such it marks an important step in the institutionalization of the genre as a standard topic of scholarly research, even as the genre itself is being called into question.

Selbmann begins with a brief sketch of the concept of *Bildung* and then traces the history of the Bildungsroman as it emerged in the works of Blanckenburg, Morgenstern, Hegel, and Dilthey. He moves on to brief discussions of major German novels written in the past two centuries that have been associated with the tradition of the Bildungsroman. Interpretations of particular novels tend to be sensitive to the problematic aspects of the works as one hero after the next either attains integration into society at the cost of considerable personal resignation or achieves personal fulfillment only in a poetic realm far removed from the society shared by author and reader. As in his earlier *Theater im Roman* (1981), Selbmann hesitates to use the term *Bildungsroman* for any other novel than *Wilhelm Meisters Lehrjahre*, which he discusses "als Muster der Gattung" [as the genre's paradigm] (63).

To this extent Selbmann codifies previous scholarship in an unpretentious but useful volume meant to guide readers through the bewildering profusion of Bildungsroman criticism. More ambitious is his own attempt to redefine the genre. Noting the historical gap between alleged examples of the genre and its introduction into the critical vocabulary, Selbmann observes astutely that familiar definitions of the Bildungsroman seem better suited to describe works of popular fiction than serious literature. He develops his theory of the genre by distinguishing among *Bildungsstruktur*, *Bildungsgeschichte*, and Bildungsroman. The first term refers to the smallest building blocks of the novel structure thematically related to the concept of *Bildung* (39). The novel becomes a *Bildungsgeschichte* when the entire work takes *Bildung* as its central theme. Such works cannot occur before the late eighteenth century. Nevertheless, Selbmann insists that the *Bildungsgeschichte* only becomes a Bildungsroman when it asserts its claim to being the binding authority ["verbindliche Instanz"] of the entire novel (40). Exactly how this notion differs from the previous definition of the *Bildungsgeschichte* as a thematiza- tion of *Bildung* throughout the entire text (39) remains unclear. It would seem that Selbmann adopts the category of the *Bildungsgeschichte* to avoid having to identify overly problematic or pessimistic novels as examples of the Bil- dungsroman. In my opinion, the notion found in the work of Martin Swales and Klaus-Dieter Sorg of an inherently self-critical genre renders this strategy superfluous.

Selbmann summarizes the main points of his monograph in the introduc- tion to an anthology of historically significant articles on the Bildungsroman (1988). The collection itself is extremely useful, as Selbmann brings together several texts that were previously inaccessible — in particular three essays by Karl Morgenstern. The decision to republish these and other articles marks an important development in the study of the Bildungsroman as attention shifts away from the novels and toward the history of the genre as a topic of critical discourse.

Dennis F. Mahoney gives a succinct overview of Bildungsroman criticism in his history of the German novel around 1800 (1988). He cites critics who question whether the genre was really as widespread and important as it had previously seemed but maintains that we should not abandon the Bildungsro- man. Here and in a more recent article Mahoney proposes that "instead of attempting to define the novels of Goethe and the German Romantics accord- ing to their content," we should "consider their intended effect upon the reader" (1991, 100). The major novelists of the period sought to create alert readers for their demanding literary works. Unfortunately, however, the public found the novels increasingly inaccessible, and the writers became "instrumental in creating the rigid division between 'high' and 'low' culture" particularly "typical of German intellectual life" (117). Here Mahoney echoes the charge that reading the Bildungsroman soon became a rewarding but unpleasant cultural chore: "Zur Aufgabe wurde die Romanlektüre, nicht unbedingt zum Vergnügen" (1988, 54). Making a virtue out of necessity, he maintains that the very complexity that made the novels unpopular at the time of their appearance has encouraged "their critical rediscovery in the past few decades" (1991, 116).

Jürgen Jacobs and Markus Krause collaborated on a study of the Bildungs-roman for the series *Arbeitsbücher zur Literaturgeschichte* [Workbooks on Literary History] in 1989. Like Selbmann's 1984 volume, the work provides a critical survey of the topic for both student and scholar. The book is divided into five sections, beginning with the history of the genre in literary criticism and moving to sections on the Enlightenment, the Age of Goethe, and the nineteenth and twentieth centuries. Each section contains a briefly annotated bibliography followed by a sketch of the intellectual and political climate of a given period. Seven novels receive thorough discussion, with particular attention to areas of critical controversy: *Agathon*, *Wilhelm Meisters Lehrjahre*, *Heinrich von Ofterdingen*, *Titan*, *Nachsommer*, *Der grüne Heinrich*, and *Der Zauberberg*. Krause contributed the sections on the nine-teenth century and the literature of the Federal Republic; Jacobs wrote the rest.

The introductory nature of the volume compels the authors to survey familiar territory. Jacobs' and Krause's work improves on earlier studies in several ways, however: the bibliography is more up to date and considerably more extensive, as are the discussions of individual novels. The section on the twentieth-century Bildungsroman has been greatly expanded over Selbmann's brief comments, including sections on postwar novels in both the German Democratic Republic and the Federal Republic. While both handbooks offer valuable insights into individual texts, Jacobs and Krause give a better sense of interpretive debates surrounding the novels. Unlike Selbmann, they do not attempt to define the Bildungsroman in a new way, nor do they attempt to rename the genre.

Instead, the authors turn back to Dilthey's influential definition of the Bildungsroman:

Es empfiehlt sich, mit ihm [dem Begriff des Bildungsromans] lediglich die Vorstellung zu verbinden, daß der Entwicklungsgang einer zen-tralen Figur erzählt wird, der über bald bereichernde, bald desillusi-onierende Erfahrungen zur Selbstfindung und zum Eintreten in bejahte Bindungen führt. (20)

[It is advisable to associate {the concept of the Bildungsroman} simply with the narration of a central figure's course of development through sometimes enriching, sometimes disillusioning experiences to self-discovery and entry into affirmed social obligations.]

In contrast to some critics, Jacobs and Krause are willing to extend the term to cover both German novels written in the twentieth century and works in other national literatures. Before long, however, their "liberal" concept of the genre (18) turns out to be quite conservative. *Agathon*, *Titan*, and *Der Zauberberg* are only reluctantly included in the exclusive list of German *Bildungsromane*. *Heinrich von Ofterdingen* qualifies only as an unusual case, as does *Der Nachsommer*, which features as "a problematic exception to the rule" (173). Both *Hyperion* (72) and *Der grüne Heinrich* (191) turn out to be *Desillusionsromane*, while *Anton Reiser* (51), *Stopfkuchen* (155), and *Die Blechtrommel* (231) are listed as *Antibildungsromane*.

We are left, not surprisingly, with *Wilhelm Meisters Lehrjahre*. Here Jacobs wages a vigorous campaign against an increasing number of critics, including Karl Schlechta, Heinz Schlaffer, Guiliano Baioni, Klaus-Dieter Sorg and Jochen Hörisch, who question the exemplary nature of Meister's *Bildung* and the seemingly happy ending of the novel. Jacobs accuses Sorg of having an "allergic reaction" to any form of discipline imposed on Wilhelm Meister, and dismisses other works in this critical vein as anachronistic attempts to impose late-twentieth-century subjectivism on an eighteenth-century text (79-80). The "correct" interpretation of Goethe's novel is irrelevant in this context; of interest is what the exchange reveals about Jacobs's understanding of the genre as a whole. Despite generous gestures at the outset, it becomes increasingly clear that he and Krause are working with a one-novel genre that has a handful of deviant brothers and a few distant relatives. Once again Swales and Sorg suggest an understanding of the genre that could accommodate more texts with less agonizing.

Terminological quibbles aside, Jacobs and Krause do produce a series of excellent critical assessments of novels associated with *Wilhelm Meisters Lehrjahre*. They point out that any effort to discuss the pertinent secondary literature necessarily involves some selectivity, but in my view two seem particularly regrettable. The authors do not discuss the relation of the now-canonical Bildungsromane to the so-called *Trivialliteratur* that was more popular when the novels were written. More attention to both the dynamics of canon formation and the relation between popular narrative forms and the Bildungsroman would have been welcome. A second and related concern involves the near complete absence of texts by or about women (Christa Wolf is the exception) and the total neglect of poststructuralist and feminist studies of the relation between gender and genre in the Bildungsroman. Although the authors digest vast amounts of recent scholarship, their selection is governed by the same concerns that guided Jacobs's study of Wilhelm Meister and his brothers in 1972. In this regard the work proves disappointing — an authoritative, up-to-date anachronism.

James N. Hardin provides an informed introduction to the Bildungsroman for an English-speaking audience in the anthology *Reflection and Action* (1991). Hardin observes in his introduction to the volume that the term has gained widespread currency among critics outside of German studies who remain largely ignorant of the debates surrounding the genre in its native land. Most of the essays are not new, but they are more recent than those republished by Selbmann (1988), and many appear in English for the first time. Hardin's title sums up "the two poles of the Bildungsroman." The protagonist must act. Indeed, it "is his enthusiasm, his naive vigor, his energy and drive that are attractive and that maintain the interest of the reader in him." At the same time, however, both protagonist and reader must pause to reflect on "the development of mind and soul" (xiii). Hardin sketches the genre's history, with welcome attention to recent feminist debates about the Bildungsroman.

The anthology includes seminal essays by Martini (1961), Swales (1978b) and Steinecke (1984). In addition, Jeffrey Sammons updates his reflections on the nineteenth-century German novel in a new essay. He again challenges the common assumptions that the Bildungsroman is a peculiarly German genre and that it was the dominant form of the nineteenth-century German novel, and he cautions against the indiscriminate use of the term by those outside of German studies. Most of the remaining essays, which focus on individual texts, set out to prove that the works are *not* Bildungsromane, at least not in the traditional sense of the term. To those who have followed the German debate in recent decades this skepticism will not come as a surprise, but it may introduce a note of caution into the work of those outside the narrow confines of *Germanistik* who have eagerly embraced the term.

Gerhard Mayer's monumental study of the German Bildungsroman (1992) is the most comprehensive survey of the genre since Jürgen Jacobs's *Wilhelm Meister und seine Brüder* (1972). Beginning with an overview of the concept of *Bildung* and the genre's prehistory, he surveys novels from Wieland's *Agathon* and Goethe's *Wilhelm Meisters Lehrjahre* to the present. The sheer size and scope of the volume announce the author's ambition to produce the definitive history of Bildungsroman for some time to come. The attempt is only partially successful.

Unlike Jacobs, who concluded that the Bildungsroman was an "unfulfilled genre," Mayer extends the term to dozens of German texts and even a few works of British and American fiction. He bases his understanding of the genre on a structural model that serves as a minimal checklist to identify common features in works that vary in accordance with particular historical situations. These features include a belief in the "Bildsamkeit des Individuums," that is, an ability on the part of the protagonist to develop toward a sense of personal identity through interaction with the surrounding world (19).

Additional characteristics of the genre include a chronologically ordered narrative focused on a single protagonist, the subordination of other characters to this figure, and a didactically motivated narrator.

Mayer is able to find more examples of the Bildungsroman than Jacobs because he is willing to include aesthetically inferior works that fit the basic pattern, and because he does not require that the author lead his hero to a happy ending. For example, he argues that Keller's *Der grüne Heinrich* fits the structural model of the genre despite the pessimism of the first version and the resignation of the second. For novels that go still further in inverting the optimistic premises of the genre, Mayer reserves the term *Antibildungsroman*. Mayer first defined this subgenre in an article published in 1974. He includes such novels as Hoffmann's *Kater Murr*, Raabe's *Stopfkuchen*, and Grass's *Die Blechtrommel*. These works serve as a critical corrective to the deficits of contemporary concepts of *Bildung* (66). In Mayer's view, the Antibildungsroman does not come after the Bildungsroman but accompanies it from the outset (409). This contention enables him to avoid the familiar narrative of the "rise and fall" of the German Bildungsroman and to depict a genre that displays critical self-awareness from its beginnings.

The greatest strength of Mayer's study lies in its encyclopedic range. As one would expect, he surveys major works of the German Romantics and Realists and such twentieth-century authors as Thomas Mann, Hermann Hesse, and Günter Grass. But Mayer also includes sections on many lesser-known authors and texts, as well as extensive discussions of the socialist Bildungsroman in the former German Democratic Republic and the fascist Bildungsroman of the Third Reich. Many readers will be surprised to learn that Joseph Goebbels — a former Germanist — was the author of a Bildungsroman entitled *Michael* (1929) before moving on to greater notoriety in the political realm.

When Mayer covers more familiar territory the results are considerably less interesting. He offers cogent summaries of the standard line on well-known authors and periods, but readers in search of innovative interpretations will have to look elsewhere. As Mayer points out in his preface, the broad scope of the survey makes it impossible for him to engage more than a handful of major critics. The unfortunate result is the silencing of the many voices that have enlivened recent study of the Bildungsroman, whether they be feminist, new historicist, psychoanalytic, or poststructuralist. Mayer serves up the Germanistic equivalent of comfort food, nonthreatening repetitions of familiar fare.

The form of the individual interpretations also leaves something to be desired. In accordance with his attempt to produce a structural model of the Bildungsroman, Mayer concludes the discussion of each novel by pointing out that it evidences both the "trans-epochal constants of the Bildungsroman" and also variable characteristics specific to particular periods or authors. He then methodically checks off those traits that qualify the novel as a Bildungsroman and summarizes its unique features. The result is tedious but at least informative; it becomes exasperating only when the reader begins to notice that Mayer repeats the same summarizing phrases verbatim in nearly every segment of his book. Self-quotation reaches absurd levels toward the end of the text: at one point Mayer begins three consecutive paragraphs with slightly altered versions of the same sentence (384-85), a sentence that soon recurs three more times on a single page (389). This mechanical style detracts needlessly from the wealth of information in this volume. While individual readings often lack originality, they combine to produce an impressive overview of a genre prone to ideological abuse but also capable of enlightened critique.

Poststructuralism, Psychoanalysis, and the Bildungsroman

Friedrich A. Kittler revolutionizes the study of the Bildungsroman in his long essay "Über die Sozialisation Wilhelm Meisters" [On the Socialization of Wilhelm Meister] (1978). For all their difference in nuance, previous critics worked largely within the interpretive parameters established by Goethe's contemporaries. Kittler's work is the first study of the genre that reflects the "paradigm shift" of poststructuralist philosophy. As David E. Wellbery observes in his introduction to Kittler's more recent *Discourse Networks*, Kittler does not write "about post-structuralism," nor does he "take post-structuralism as [his] theme"; instead his work "presupposes post-structuralist thought, makes that thought the operating equipment, the hardware, with which [he] sets out to accomplish [his] own research program" (1990, viii).

Kittler revises previous understandings of the self, the family, and the social function of literature. We recall that the emergence of the Bildungsroman depended on a notion of the self as something that enters into the world with innate potential and then unfolds in the course of life experience. Kittler, in contrast, defines the self as an empty space that is constructed by its initiation into discourse. Kittler's "discourse analysis" therefore presupposes

> daß die Menschen nicht in ein Universum von Gegebenheiten, sondern in ein Universum von Diskursen eintreten, die Ich und Welt, Traum und Wirklichkeit, Trug und Wahrheit erst voneinander scheiden und damit erschaffen. (7)

[that people do not enter a universe of given facts, but rather a universe of discourses that separate self and world, dream and reality, deception and truth from one another and thereby create them.]

Whereas Freudian psychoanalysis still views the individual as a site of conflicting natural impulses, Kittler argues, with Jacques Lacan, that these drives are a product of cultural discourses (12). Discursive socialization replaces organic *Bildung*.

Mothers play a central role in the socialization of their children, argues Kittler, but this was not always the case. In the course of the eighteenth century we witness the gradual transformation of the extended *Großfamilie* into the nuclear *Kleinfamilie*. Mother, father, and children remain at the center of a family structure that had once embraced the older generation, relatives, and servants. Moreover, the father, who had once worked together with the family in the home, now goes out to perform his professional duties as a civil servant (*Beamter*). The isolated mothers develop new intimacy with their children, who become the focal point of the family. During the Enlightenment, Kittler argues, education (*Erziehung*) was the task of the father; now the mother takes over the task of "primary socialization," which takes the form of *Bildung*. An identification of mother with the (male) child replaces paternal pedagogy. Kittler maintains that this "matrilinear recoding" of the family is more deeply revolutionary than the political upheavals of the epoch; we witness the emergence of the nuclear family of the middle class, which produces the socially productive individual (7).

Kittler develops his theory through an intricate reading of the *Lehrjahre*. He locates the shift from the extended to the nuclear family in the rewriting of the *Sendung* into the *Lehrjahre*. The formerly promiscuous mother now centers her attention on Wilhelm. She gives him the puppets that she loves and thereby establishes their mutual enthusiasm for the theater. "Ihr Bezug zum Sohn ist Identifikation" [She relates to her son through identification] (23). Later mother and son eagerly supplement their remembrance of the past in an erotically charged narrative that reveals both the sexualization of childhood and their discourse (30). Wilhelm's lover Mariane, however, comes from a different social milieu that has not yet witnessed the transformation of the family. Hence, when Meister reenacts the Oedipal situation with Mariane by telling her at great length about his childhood love for the theater that has brought him to her bed, she simply falls asleep.

During the final books of the novel Wilhelm undergoes a "secondary socialization" through his initiation into the Tower Society. Primary socialization takes place orally between mothers and sons; secondary socialization inscribes the individual into a patriarchal world of writing. Among the archives of the Tower Society Meister finds his own biography. The perception of himself as literature turns him into an author as he paraphrases the Tower Society's text in an autobiographical letter in which he proposes to Therese. Here Kittler adopts Michel Foucault's unconventional notion of authorship, whereby the discourse invents the author and not the other way around. Socialization culminates with the individual's entry into the discourse network of literature ("das Aufschreibesystem Literatur") (106). Wilhelm "hört auf, ein Held von Begebenheiten zu sein, und wird zum Kettenglied einer Maschine, die Diskurse produziert, distribuiert und konsumiert" [ceases to be a hero of events and becomes a cog in a machine that produces, distributes, and consumes discourses] (107). At this point Wilhelm Meister has completed his movement from the private sphere of the home into the public realm of writing and literature (on authorship see Foucault 1977, 137-38).

Kittler's discourse-analytical conception of *Bildung* leads to a new understanding of literature and the Bildungsroman. The work of literature becomes a metadiscourse — "ein Diskurs über Diskurse" (8) — that goes beyond the reflection of reality to the production of reality: "ein diskursives Ereignis, d.h. ... eine Rede, die in ihrem Ergehen etwas tut, statt nur in ihren Inhalten etwas zu bedeuten" [a discursive event, that is ... a discourse that does something as it comes out, rather than merely to mean something in its content] (7). What literature "does" is to complete the process of socialization, and the product of this symbiosis is the Bildungsroman: "der Bildungsroman [koppelt] Sozialisation und Literatur" [the Bildungsroman {links} socialization and literature] (108). The relentless archival activity of the Tower Society combines techniques of writing and power that create individuals as a product of social discipline. The literature that creates Wilhelm Meister as an author, in turn, functions to create new readers and writers in the reception of *Wilhelm Meisters Lehrjahre*. "Der Bildungsroman als Paradigma der Kunst, Bücher zu lesen, ist eine Sozialisationstechnik ... Der 'Mensch' wird Grund und Sache der Diskurse" [As a paradigm of the art of reading books, the Bildungsroman is a socialization technique .... "Man" becomes the foundation and the subject matter of the discourses] (112; on social discipline see Foucault 1979, 250).

The uncompromising difficulty of Kittler's prose and the originality of his approach limited his immediate influence on the study of the Bildungsroman. For example, surveys of the genre by Selbmann and by Jacobs and Krause simply ignore the existence of his work. Although Kittler displays a solid knowledge of previous scholarship on *Wilhelm Meisters Lehrjahre*, he moves boldly into a realm that divorces him from that tradition. Certainly part of the reason for his initial obscurity lies in the belated reception of poststructuralist thought in Germany. While his work assumes intimate familiarity with the work of Foucault, Lacan, and Jacques Derrida, criticism in Germany in 1978 was dominated by reception theory and Theodor Adorno-inspired *Ideologie-*

kritik. Two aspects of Kittler's work deserve particular notice for their bearing on future studies: first, he incorporates the question of gender into his study of the Bildungsroman. Previous critics had tacitly assumed that *Bildung* was at least theoretically open to all around 1800, whereas Kittler argues that it functioned to prepare only men for their roles as authors and civil servants. He nevertheless leaves open the question of how to account for those women writers who published despite widespread prejudice. The historical restriction of *Bildung* to men becomes of central interest in studies of women's writing and the female Bildungsroman during the 1980s. Second, Kittler's understanding of literature as a metadiscourse challenges the concept of aesthetic autonomy. He rejects the neat separation between art and life and views literature as a reflection on the discourses that constitute individuals as part of the public sphere.

Dorothea E. von Mücke builds on Kittler's foundation in her study of "Generic Innovation and the Pedagogical Project in Eighteenth-Century Literature" (1991). Mücke investigates "the socializing function of poetic illusion" and contends that the emergence of new literary genres can be interpreted in terms of changes within the "aesthetic-pedagogical program" of the eighteenth century (6-7). The mid century witnessed the rise of the epistolary novel and the bourgeois tragedy in response to a demand for aesthetic transparency or *Anschaulichkeit*. Such writings and performances encourage readers or spectators to forget that they are consuming a work of art and to identify completely with the seeming reality of the representation. Mücke develops this concept through a close reading of the semiotic theories of Condillac, Lessing, and Diderot and applies it to the analysis of Richardson's *Clarissa* (1747-48) and Lessing's *Miß Sara Sampson* (1755). Both drama and novel elicit an emotional response of pity that makes them effective for the moral improvement of society. Central to Mücke's understanding of the eighteenth century is Michel Foucault's contention that it witnessed a transformation in the way the state asserted its authority over its subjects. Punishment based on public spectacle yielded to a form of private discipline that imprinted social values onto individual minds (1979). Mücke argues that the new aesthetics of *Anschaulichkeit* reflect this transformation, or rather, that the new genres it inspires play an active role in the production of "new types of subjectivity" (11). In short, "the anti-theatrical literary genres of the age of transparency are conceived primarily as instruments for disciplining the male bourgeois subject" (15).

Mücke identifies the beginnings of a new aesthetic-pedagogical program in the work of Rousseau that will lead to the "project of *Bildung*" (161). In *Julie ou la Nouvelle Héloïse* (1761) we witness "the disciplining of desire, the taming of the masculine imagination, through the construction of the ideal Woman in the epistolary novel" (154). It was only with Wieland's *Agathon*, however, that the new genre of the Bildungsroman emerged. Here Mücke identifies a shift away from the aesthetic transparency to aesthetic distance. Hallucinatory empathy with the other turns to narcissistic self-reflection (204). Agathon stabilizes his sense of self not through experience alone but through the narration of a coherent story that produces his identity (244). Whereas writers in England, France, and Germany had shared in the pedagogical project of the aesthetics of transparency, Mücke argues that the Bildungsroman was restricted to Germany. Its purpose was to produce male civil servants. In this context she challenges the concept of aesthetic autonomy and resists the notion that the ideal of *Bildung* constitutes "a compensatory or utopian project vis-à-vis the social and political changes of that period; rather, it participated in exactly those transformations in subject formation and the reorganization of discursive fields" (191).

David Roberts offers a significant contribution to Bildungsroman criticism in his psychoanalytical study of the *Lehrjahre* (1980). Rather than hunting for phallic symbols in the mode of early Freudian criticism, Roberts links psychoanalysis to the narrative structure of Goethe's novel, which he then relates to its social context. He notes at the outset that in moving from the *Sendung* to the *Lehrjahre* Goethe has transformed Meister's theatrical mission into a mistake that nevertheless indirectly leads him "to an unforeseen social goal" (10). Roberts then pursues two related questions: "what is the meaning of the hero's detour to his goal," and "what is the *structure* of relations which articulates the integration of the theatrical mission ... into the overall plan of the novel?" (11).

Roberts views Meister's development as an overcoming of Oedipal conflict symbolized by the painting of "Der kranke Königssohn" [the sick son of the king] in his father's home, which represents a boy witnessing his father's second marriage. Through his analysis of *Hamlet* in the *Lehrjahre* Meister indirectly works through his own Oedipal desires; acting out the role on stage "releases him from the spell of the tragedy" (29). Once cured, Meister can assume his roles as father of Felix and as Natalie's husband. Seen in terms of the structure of the novel itself, the *Hamlet* interpretation sublates (*hebt auf*) the *Sendung* into the *Lehrjahre*, which is to say that it makes it into a Bildungsroman. "This process of self-integration ... is equally of course the process of social integration," and Roberts views the Bildungsroman "as the symbolic form of this twofold constitution of the subject" (16). Wilhelm Meister's own "cure" that leads to a reconciliation with the father

> registers — post-Italy and in the wake of the French Revolution — the necessity of advancing beyond the failed rebellion of the Sturm und Drang generation by seeking ... a reforming alliance between bourgeois commerce and feudal-aristocratic landed property. (25-26)

Thus, Roberts combines psychoanalysis and social history in a meticulously close reading of *Hamlet* in the *Lehrjahre*. The result is a different type of understanding of the Bildungsroman in its social context. While Schlaffer found history in the failed resolution of textual problems, Roberts insists on Meister's successful cure but views this cure as a symbol of theodicy (19), an allegory of the sociopolitical aspirations of Weimar Classicism.

At approximately the same time Adolf Muschg and Gerhard Kaiser published significant psychoanalytical studies of Gottfried Keller and his autobiographical novel *Der grüne Heinrich*. Muschg centers his study around the concept of *Schuld*, understood in the double sense of personal guilt and financial debt. He begins with a Freudian analysis of Keller. In the typical Oedipal family the boy unconsciously views the father as a rival for his mother's affection and wishes for the father's death. In Keller's case the unconscious desire was realized, however, for his father died when Keller was only five years old. This childhood trauma left Keller with a sense of guilt that makes it impossible for him to grow up. He remained trapped in the Oedipal bond to his mother, while the father assumed the position of an absent deity. Keller remained financially and emotionally tied to his mother throughout his life: he exploited her for years in pursuit of a failed career as a landscape painter and never married. In Muschg's view, Keller's multifaceted indebtedness became a motivating force throughout his life. *Schuld* is a sign of a deficit, a lack, and hence becomes a source of labor to correct it. For Keller, then, guilt/debt serve as the "motor of socialization;" he strove to transform *Schuld* into social obligation [*Schuldigkeit*] (1977, 39-41). Keller paid off his debt in two ways: for some fifteen years he worked as an exceptionally conscientious civil servant for the Swiss government, a career Muschg views as an expression of loss for his failed course of personal development [*Bildungsgang*] (285). Before and after this self-imposed punishment Keller wrote. His autobiographical novel reveals the burden of guilt that made it impossible for him to become a man. As Renate Voris observes, Muschg's insistence that Keller did *not* develop constitutes the primary innovation of his biography (1983). She points out that Emil Ermatinger had imposed the classical notion of *Bildung* onto Keller's life, insisting that it led to harmony between the *Weltseele* [world-soul] and the individual *Geist* [spirit] (285). In contrast, Muschg denies the teleology of a developing identity: "Muschgs Keller entwickelt sich überhaupt nicht" [Muschg's Keller does not develop at all] (297). Each chapter of Muschg's biography revolves around the same point: Keller's relationship to his mother and his (absent) father.

Some four years later Gerhard Kaiser published a monumental study of Keller's oeuvre that expands on the basic premises of Muschg's psychoanalytic approach (1981). Kaiser stresses the interconnection between Keller's life and work, viewing *Der grüne Heinrich* as something between autobiography and fiction. Here the narcissistic author turns a sense of personal lack into the source of artistic creativity as an invented life compensates for real loss (31). Kaiser argues that Keller's need to invent his autobiography stemmed from the lack of a father that made him unfit for bourgeois life (39). Like Muschg, Kaiser argues that the loss of the father in mid-Oedipal crisis at age five fulfilled a wish to remove the rival and at the same time created guilt: the son who desired the mother became a parricide. In addition, the son lost the mentor who would have guided him to manhood. Kaiser goes beyond Muschg by situating Keller's personal crisis in its historical context. As he observes, the Oedipal conflict evident in Keller's life and work is a product of the nuclear family that emerged in the eighteenth century: the ancient King Oedipus did not have an Oedipal complex (55). Kaiser goes on to argue that the classical Bildungsroman grows out of the new nuclear family and the contrasting gender roles ascribed to men and women. The woman is to stay at home and tend the children while the man ventures forth into the public sphere. Together the parents mold the inner emotional life of the child and prepare him (*sic*) to enter the outer world. The successful product of maternal nurture in the home and paternal introduction into society is the psychologically balanced and socially integrated individual whose development is the theme of the classical Bildungsroman (48). But Heinrich lacks a father, which stunts his development. He remains in the grasp of his mother, who, as an incarnation of the mythical powers of nature represents both womb and tomb — the source of life but also a deadly force that pulls him into the grave (60).

The basic Oedipal conflict determines the failed course of Heinrich's development. He is expelled from school as an adolescent. The school is a paternal institution that prepares the child for public life, but Heinrich is forced to return to the maternal sphere; he is not permitted to become a father (76). As an adolescent Heinrich displaces his desire for his mother into a tender love for the sickly blond Anna and barely repressed passion for the lusty brunette Judith. Near the end of the novel it seems that he will succeed in his path to maturity after all. After a long fruitless stay in Munich the penniless failed artist resolves to walk back to his mother in Switzerland. An enlightened aristocrat shelters the young man. It seems that everything is about to turn out for the best: the duke pays Heinrich handsomely for his collected drawings and paintings, commissions additional work, adopts him as a son, and seems favorably inclined to a marriage between Heinrich and his adopted daughter. Kaiser points out that the duke occupies a position in the novel analogous to that of the Tower Society in Goethe's *Lehrjahre*. Yet the parallel soon breaks down: whereas the Tower Society confirms Wilhelm's paternity of the child Felix and assures his marriage to the noble Natalie, Heinrich's potential happiness is not realized. The entire episode has the quality of a dream that unfortunately enables Heinrich to repress the memory of his poor sick mother in Switzerland (136-37). Heinrich returns home filled with hope of marriage and enthusiasm for his democratic country. In his first act of solidarity with the community he joins a church service — only to discover to his shock that it is the funeral of his mother, who has died a pathetic death in his absence. The devastated son withers away and dies in the first version of the novel; in the second he survives as a melancholy bachelor civil servant. Thus, Kaiser concludes that *Der grüne Heinrich* takes back the historical postulate of the Bildungsroman; it is closer to Karl Philipp Moritz's *Anton Reiser* than the *Lehrjahre* (137). It is precisely Keller's rejection of a facile happiness for his hero that constitutes the strength of the novel. Heinrich cannot escape his past: "Der keinen Vater hat, wird kein Vater werden" [He who has no father will never become a father] (149).

Jochen Hörisch combines Lacanian psychology with Marxist economic theory in his study of Goethe's *Lehrjahre*, Keller's *Der grüne Heinrich*, and Mann's *Der Zauberberg* (1983). He argues that the alleged authenticity of the self and its autonomous development in the Bildungsroman is a falsification of literary history by the institution of *Germanistik*. The subject is not an originary presence but rather an effect of signifying structures. In his view, the great Bildungsromane hardly describe *Bildung* as a gradual process of enriching self-development; instead, they trace the history of subjects drained of their vitality (241). Hörisch traces a downward spiral of increasing impoverishment from Goethe to Mann, measured in terms of the steady collapse of the nuclear family. While Kittler had documented the origins of bourgeois identity at the end of the eighteenth century, Hörisch narrates the history of its gradual demise in the course of the nineteenth.

Already in the *Lehrjahre*, Hörisch says, we see evidence of repression. Meister leaves an originally intact family behind to found a surrogate family composed of himself, Natalie, and his son Felix. For Hörisch as for Roberts, the *Hamlet* performance marks the turning point of the novel, as it initiates Meister into the symbolic order of the father. Meister's success comes dear, however, as the construction of his new family requires the sacrifice of those such as the Harpist and Mignon who refuse to submit to the symbolic order. In this context Hörisch writes of Goethe's "inhuman, indeed, anti-human novel" (77). Hörisch moves from Lacanian psychoanalysis to Marxist theory in his study of Keller. Exchange value replaced use value in the nineteenth century, and the principle of equivalency reduced objects to commodities. This development disappointed the expected development of the self: the emancipation of the subject from the feudal order resulted only in new bondage to work, capital, and exchange. The central theme of *Der grüne Heinrich* is, therefore, the loss of immediacy through exchange-compulsion [*Tausch-*

zwang] (139). The novel presents an inflationary decoupling of truth, identity, and equivalence.

Hörisch concludes with a discussion of eroticism and death in Richard Wagner's *Tristan und Isolde* (1865) and Mann's *Der Zauberberg*. Like Kittler, he writes for the initiate and lards his text with extensive citations of poststructuralist theory. At best this practice creates a dense texture of cross-references between current thought and earlier literature. Too often interpretation proceeds through free association, however, and the technique of citing several writers in each sentence becomes tiresome. On a thematic level, Hörisch risks falling into a contradiction typical of poststructuralist thought. On the one hand, he polemicizes against mystified readers who have been seduced into belief in the organic self. On the other hand, however, his own argument traces a familiar narrative of historical decline and voices a pathos-filled lament for lost subjectivity.

Hans-Jürgen Schings also adopts a psychological approach in his study of the "pathogenesis of the modern subject in the Bildungsroman" (1984). Schings locates the birth of modern subjectivity in the late eighteenth century; it is a birth that he describes as painful, signaled by crisis and sickness. It is in response to this crisis of modern subjectivity that the Bildungsroman appears: "Der *Bildungsroman* ist die Antwort auf eine Pathogenese .... Nicht *Bildung*, sondern zuvörderst Therapie gewinnt mithin fundamentale Bedeutung" [The *Bildungsroman* is the answer to a pathogenesis .... It is not primarily *Bildung*, but rather therapy that gains fundamental importance] (45).

Schings then traces the emergence of the subject in novels by Wieland, Moritz, and Goethe. Each protagonist exhibits a specific form of pathological subjectivity: Agathon *Milzsucht* (spleen), Anton Reiser melancholy and egotism, Wilhelm Meister hypochondria. Cured once of his *Schwärmerei* [excessive sentimentality], Agathon needs a second corrective to turn his misanthropy into a modest skepticism. Moritz can diagnose the circumstances that prohibited his own personal development in *Anton Reiser*, but he cannot find a cure. Wilhelm Meister, in contrast, is healed (55). His development necessarily entails painful sacrifice, but in the end his newly acquired subjectivity remains intact. In the course of his Bildungsroman he learns to direct his attention to the external world, which heals his pathological inwardness. New and noteworthy in Sching's approach is the interest in eighteenth-century psychopathology: rather than imposing Freudian or post-Freudian terminology onto the past, he views the works in the context of the psychological discourse that was developing in the late eighteenth century. The interpretation of the *Lehrjahre* is less original, however, merely restating the affirmative understanding of the novel in psychological terminology.

Norbert Ratz makes use of Erik Erikson's social psychology in the analysis of what he terms the *Identitätsroman* [identity novel] (1988). After surveying the problematic status of *Bildungsroman* and considering other terms that have been suggested in its place, Ratz decides that his own coinage best expresses the common factor in novels ranging from Grimmelshausen's *Simplicissimus* to Mann's *Zauberberg*. Each protagonist is said to strive toward "ego identity" [*Ich-Identität*], a key concept in Erikson's work that involves developing a sense of personal identity in a particular social context. An adolescent crisis precipitated by the conflict between the protagonist's sense of self and social expectations — *Identitätsverwirrung* — leads to *Selbstreflexion* and finally to *Synthetisierung*, in which childhood patterns of identification are revised in the light of personal experience and social expectations. By analyzing the works in terms of their varied presentation of the hero's movement through this three-stage pattern of psychological development, Ratz claims to determine a common narrative structure of novels hitherto categorized on the basis of their content.

To Ratz's credit, theoretical concepts are used as a heuristic device, not an interpretive straightjacket. The theory is broad enough to account for a wide variety of literary texts, and Ratz readily admits that individual novels may well not follow precisely the three stages; indeed, the absence of a final synthesis is often particularly significant. Novels tend to fall into two broad categories: fragmentary works that portray the protagonists' inability to attain *Ich-Identität*, and completed texts that depict either a flawed or unattainable utopia. Novels by Grimmelshausen, Moritz, Jean Paul, and Mann belong to the first group; works by Wieland, Goethe, and Stifter to the second.

Given the tendency toward taxonomic proliferation that the Bildungsroman inspires, it seems unlikely that Ratz's contribution will gain universal acceptance. Like the term it seeks to supplant, the broadness of the concept of ego-identity that enables Ratz to discuss novels spanning nearly three centuries threatens to undermine its alleged precision. While there is much to be said for Ratz's decision to view a standard list of German novels through a particular theoretical perspective, his project does not seem to warrant renaming the entire genre in accordance with his own interpretive preoccupations. The strength of the book lies rather in his nuanced readings of individual texts, readings that remain consistently sensitive to the novels' complexity and their authors' avoidance of unconvincing happy endings.

If questions regarding the status of heterosexual relations in the Bildungsroman received little attention until fairly recently, it is hardly surprising that homosexuality has been almost completely ignored. Two essays have begun to open up a field of inquiry that is almost certain to receive more attention in coming years. In 1985 Karl Werner Böhm published a study of "the homosexual elements in Thomas Mann's *Der Zauberberg*." Interest in the topic of Mann's own repressed homoerotic desires had been fanned by the publication of his diaries a few years earlier, but Böhm is particularly interested in the symbolic function of homosexuality within the novel. The first half of *Der Zauberberg* portrays what Böhm terms Hans Castorp's "re-homosexualization" as his infatuation for the Russian woman Claudia Chauchat on the magic mountain releases the repressed memory of his adolescent attraction to a Slavic boy named Pribislav Hippe. When Chauchat leaves the sanatorium Castorp once again represses his homosexual desires in the name of an abstract idealization of bisexuality. In Böhm's view, this renewed rejection of homosexuality can be understood as an encoded expression of Mann's changing political views. Citing Mann's essay "Über die Ehe" [On Marriage], Böhm points out that Mann identifies homosexuality with sterility and death. Moreover, Mann associates homoeroticism with a glorification of male bonding in the military. Both are linked to his romantic conservatism during the war years, and thus the new affirmation of democracy goes hand in hand with a repudiation of homosexuality (163).

Robert Tobin turns his attention to the construction of gender in the classical Bildungsroman (1993). He begins with a look at the medical discourse of the late eighteenth century and discovers that physicians advocated moderate sexual activity for the purpose of establishing the "healthy" bourgeois family. In *Agathon* we witness both a sharp rejection of homosexuality and suspicion of excessive female sexuality, although Wieland stops short of bringing his hero into a conventional bourgeois family. Moritz's Anton Reiser feels a strong pull toward members of his own sex and an aversion to women, but these illicit passions only trigger his self-destructive tendencies. Only Goethe's Wilhelm Meister succeeds in completing his education and founding a family. Tobin views the process of *Bildung* portrayed in *Wilhelm Meisters Lehrjahre* as the socialization of a young man into heterosexual society. In the process Meister must repress his strong youthful homoeroticism, while sexually ambivalent individuals such as Mignon and the beautiful soul are destroyed.

Gender and Genre in the Bildungsroman

In her survey of the "Feminist Critical Revolution" Elaine Showalter identifies three phases in the development of feminist literary analysis: critics begin by "exposing the misogyny of literary practice," identifying "stereotyped images of women in literature" and calling attention to "the exclusion of women from literary history" (1985, 5). Feminists recover the suppressed tradition of women's writing in the second phase and question the possibility of a peculiarly feminine form of writing (*l'écriture féminine*) in the third. We can identify elements of each aspect of the feminist critical revolution in

recent studies of the Bildungsroman, although not necessarily in strict chronological order. Since the late 1970s critics have begun to explore gender-
related issues in the Bildungsroman that had previously been ignored.

In an early anthology of essays, *Die Frau als Heldin und Autorin* [The
Woman as Heroine and Author] (1979), Barbara Becker-Cantarino and Wulf
Köpke began to question the role of female characters in the male Bildungsroman. Whereas previous critics had celebrated the vision of sexual liberation
for both men and women in Friedrich Schlegel's *Lucinde* (1799), Becker-
Cantarino argues that Schlegel creates a male fantasy. *Bildung* is for men
only; the woman, as the embodiment of nature and lover, remains static,
significant primarily in her role as an important stage in male development
(122). For Köpke, too, the emancipated woman in the literature around 1800
appears as a fascinating possibility and potential danger in the life of the man,
whose experiences take center stage (108).

We recall that Friedrich Kittler had focused on the process of male socialization in the *Lehrjahre*. The gender roles he identified in Goethe's novel
remain constant in his wide-ranging study of German "discourse networks"
(1985). During the "Age of Goethe" the woman functions as the mother who
teaches her sons to speak and as the admiring audience for the great writer:

> In this respect the division of the sexes in the discourse network of
> 1800 was quite simple. Because the Mother produced authors as the
> unifying principle of poetic works, women had no access to any such
> unity. They remained a manifold grouped around the authorial lode-
> star. (125)

John H. Smith comes to similar conclusions in his "Sexual Difference,
Bildung, and the *Bildungsroman*" (1987). With reference to both Hegel and
Lacan, Smith defines *Bildung* as a rhetorical rather than an organic process
by which an individual develops "into a world of structures of representation"
(213). Yet not everyone has the opportunity for *Bildung*. Smith argues that

> *Bildung*, and its narrativization in the *Bildungsroman* is not an "organ-
> ic" but a social phenomenon that leads to the construction of male
> identity in our sex-gender system by granting men access to self-repre-
> sentation in the patriarchal Symbolic order. (216)

In short, "female *Bildung* [is] a contradiction in terms" (220).

Despite the cultural bias that militated against female *Bildung* and authorship, women nevertheless did write and publish during the "Age of Goethe."
How do we define the relation between novels written by women during this
period and the canonical male Bildungsroman? Some critics have emphasized

the incompatibility of the two traditions. For example, Helga Meise draws a sharp line between the male Bildungsroman and *Frauenromane* (women's novels): "Man kann sagen, daß der Bildungsroman einen neuen literarischen Diskurs eröffnet, in dem die Weiblichkeit einen anderen Platz einnimmt, der von dem der Frauenromane unterschieden ist" [One can say that the Bildungs-roman opens up a new literary discourse in which femininity occupies a different position than it does in the *Frauenromane*] (1983, 207). In Meise's view, women address the concerns of a largely female readership in works that ostensibly enforce, but also subtly undermine, the gender stereotypes disseminated in many didactic treatises of the period. More recently, Christa Bürger has argued that women writers occupied a different place in the institution of literature. Building on her earlier study (1982) of the nascent division of the literary institution into high art and popular fiction around 1800, Bürger places women writers in the "middle sphere," halfway between the didactic literature of the Enlightenment and the autonomy aesthetics of the Weimar Classicists (1990). The troubled history of the male Bildungsroman suggests another reason why some feminists might hesitate to identify its female counterpart: given the incessant terminological debates surrounding the Bildungsroman and its implication in the German ideology, why would one want to rediscover forgotten texts by women only to associate them with this dubious tradition? Finally, the search for the female Bildungsroman runs the risk of measuring women writers against a standard of male creativity. Instead of proving that women can be just as good as men, critics concentrate on "the radical Otherness of much women's writing" (Smith 1987, 221).

And yet there are novels with evolving female protagonists which many critics *are* willing to term Bildungsromane. For example, Jeannine Blackwell challenges the common assumption that the Bildungsroman is an exclusively male genre in her *"Bildungsroman mit Dame"* (1982). This unfortunately unpublished dissertation remains the most comprehensive study of the female Bildungsroman in Germany between 1770 and 1900. Blackwell defines her topic according to the gender of the protagonist rather than that of the author:

> I use the term *Bildungsroman* with respect to heroines to denote a sympathetic third person narration of the growth of one central female character from youth to the fruition of her talents, through which her internal development expresses itself outward and is in turn reshaped by the environment she affects. (14-15)

As it turns out, seven of the nine novels Blackwell examines in detail were written by women. In addition, Blackwell provides a wealth of information about women in German society and the status of the woman writer that situates each literary text in its sociohistorical context.

The didactic novels of the eighteenth century were not conducive to the female Bildungsroman because they "present a static ideal, the bourgeois woman who is an unchanging paragon of virtue" (108). Only in Sophie von LaRoche's *Geschichte des Fräulein von Sternheim* [The History of Lady Sternheim] (1771) and Friederike Helene Unger's *Julchen Grünthal* (1784) do we encounter female protagonists who develop significantly in the course of challenging experiences to find "their 'true calling'" in life (109). Yet even the happily married Sophie von Sternheim is no paragon of virtue: her actions throughout the novel "are in fact calculating and self-serving," the smug expression of a complacent conservatism (124). Julchen Grünthal is reconciled with her father at the end of the novel only by denying the experiences that have helped her mature. In this she typifies many Bildungsroman heroines: "Contrary to many *Bildungsroman* heroes, they do not apply these practical, acquired insights in their final vocations, but rather forget, suppress, or ignore them" (150; on Unger's novels and the Bildungsroman see also Heuser 1985).

Things get worse in the "novel of resignation" [*Entsagungsroman*]. Johanna Schopenhauer's *Gabriele* (1819) and Therese Huber's *Hannah, der Herrnhuterin Deborah Findling* [Hannah, the Moravian Deborah Foundling] (1821) "examine the mechanics of masochism, resignation, and voluntary celibacy as they shape personal development" (178-79). The protagonists of these novels accept the sacrifices demanded by society and yet are fully aware that their suffering serves no purpose. Religious skepticism and love have an important effect on the development of the protagonists of two Young German novels, Karl Gutzkow's *Wally die Zweiflerin* [Wally the Doubter] (1835) and Fanny Lewald's *Jenny* (1843). Wally's religious doubts lead her to "self-hate and denial of her own independence of thought" (252), while the Jewish heroine of Lewald's novel finds conversion and assimilation impossible. Her first fiancé abandons her when she confesses her reservations about his religion; years later she dies of grief when her second fiancé is mortally wounded in a duel.

Optimism returns briefly after 1848 in novels that borrow elements of the fairy tale to present "fantasies of women's emancipation" (299). The first of Eugenie Marlitt's extremely popular novels sets a pattern repeated in numerous sequels: the eponymous heroine of *Goldelse* (1866) — nicknamed for her golden hair — endures trials and tribulations before marriage to a strong, understanding man. While Marlitt glorifies the bourgeois marriage, Wilhelmine von Hellern's *Ein Arzt der Seele* [A Doctor of the Soul] (1869) portrays a woman who pursues an independent career as a scientist. Yet she, too, finds true happiness only when she agrees to marriage and motherhood. By the end of the nineteenth century fairy tales give way to detached observation sometimes bordering on clinical analysis such as one finds in Theodor

Fontane's *Mathilde Möhring* (1891-1907). Finally, Gabriele Reuter's *Aus guter Familie* [From a Good Family] (1895) combines interest in the pathological with social criticism as the heroine goes mad under the pressure to conform to socially acceptable roles.

Thus, Blackwell does not discover a series of strong, confidant heroines striding toward positions of public responsibility in her survey of the female Bildungsroman. Characters fare best when they deny their independence and submit to the demands of society. Those who do not do so risk ostracism, madness, or death. This stress on the negativity of the female experience continues in *The Voyage In*, an anthology of essays on German and English authors edited by Elizabeth Abel, Marianne Hirsch, and Elizabeth Langland (1983). In their introduction they observe that critics have consistently ignored the question of gender in studies of the Bildungsroman. In contrast, their volume "integrates gender with genre and identifies distinctively female versions of the *Bildungsroman*" (5). The editors begin with a standard, content-oriented definition of the genre that emphasizes "individual achievement and social integration" as the goals of the male Bildungsroman (5). While conceding that few texts actually fulfill these optimistic expectations, they argue that the situation is even worse for female protagonists, who "must frequently struggle to voice any aspirations whatsoever" (7).

Although the authors are careful to distinguish between the theoretical ideal of the male Bildungsroman and its considerably more problematic realizations, they nevertheless invoke the ideal on occasion to define the specific difference of the female Bildungsroman. Thus, Hirsch (1983) comments that Theodor Fontane's *Effi Briest* (1894-95) presents a "type of female plot [that] becomes a reversal of the conventional male plot, as female *Bildung* is no longer marked by progress or linear direction, but by circularity and dissolution" (42). In the introduction the editors speculate that the "fully realized and individuated self who caps the journey of the *Bildungsroman* may not represent the developmental goals of women, or of women characters" (10-11). Here we encounter the same difficulty we noted in Gerhart Mayer's discussion of the Antibildungsroman, where critics describe the specific otherness of the deviant genre on the basis of an over-simplified ideal.

For the most part, however, the authors avoid the temptation to define the female Bildungsroman solely as the negative counterpart to the male stereotype. They consider both novels in which female protagonists develop gradually and "novels of awakening," where enlightenment comes as a sudden inspiration (11-12). Sometimes appearances can be misleading: Hirsch argues against charges that the "beautiful soul" of the *Lehrjahre* retreats into neurotic isolation by claiming that her turn to inwardness and religion represent a creative response to a situation that prohibits female development. In a separate publication Susanne Zantop argues that the *Bekenntnisse einer schönen*

Seele [Confessions of a Beautiful Soul] — the fictional autobiography of a woman included in the *Lehrjahre* — reveals the impossibility for women of fulfilling both sexual desires and the desire for *Bildung* in bourgeois society. The use of religion as therapy enables the "beautiful soul" to survive. Thus, we should not view her concentration on the inner life as an expression of pure female subjectivity; rather, she constructs her identity out of foreign forms as a survival strategy in a restrictive environment (1986; on the "novel of awakening" see also Martin 1982).

Antonie Schweitzer and Simone Sitte (1985) also reveal hidden complexity in Sophie von LaRoche's *Das Fräulein von Sternheim* and Caroline von Wolzogen's *Agnes von Lilien* (1796). Both writers depict female figures intended as paragons of virtue. The characters display personal integrity and "classical simplicity" that inspires admiration and distinguishes them from stereotypes of either the bourgeois housewife or the aristocratic seductress. LaRoche's protagonist is not entirely positive, however. Pedagogy and charity give Sternheim a realm of action outside the home, but — as Blackwell had observed — in a way that does not challenge the existing social structure. In contrast, Wilhelmine Caroline von Wobeser advocates complete self-denial for women in her popular *Elisa oder das Weib wie es seyn sollte* [Elisa or Woman as She Ought to Be] (1795). Schweitzer and Sitte point out that such capitulation to restrictive norms reflects the difficulty of the woman writer, who in order to publish at all had to affirm accepted values. The authors then survey works by women writers in England and France in which models of virtue and self-sacrifice gradually yield to more realistic portrayals of rebellious heroines (see Fuderer 1990 for an extensive bibliography of the female Bildungsroman in English).

To circumvent the cultural prohibition against female creativity many women writers around 1800 published anonymously. Another strategy was to mask one's ambitions behind a male protagonist, as in the case of Dorothea Veit-Schlegel's *Florentin* (1801). As Liliane Weissberg argues, Veit-Schlegel's personal humility and her boundless admiration for both Goethe and her second husband, Friedrich Schlegel, made it difficult for her to become an author herself. She solved the problem by writing a work with a male protagonist "who cautiously tests the wishes of his mother Dorothea, and who would be able to become that man, aristocrat, and artist who truly could never have been her son." Female authorship takes the form of self-denial, in which Dorothea Schlegel becomes "submissive to her hero's wishes which she, by her own definition, would never be able to understand" (1987, 177-78).

Jeannine Blackwell brings her discussion of the female Bildungsroman up to 1900. By limiting her study to the eighteenth and nineteenth centuries she details the social conditions that made *Bildung* next to impossible for women.

In contrast, Esther Kleinbord Labovitz uses 1900 as her point of departure, as she argues that the female Bildungsroman does not occur before the twentieth century: "For the eighteenth and nineteenth century German fictional heroine, as for the real life figures, the concept of *Bildung* virtually passed her by" (1986, 4). Only in the twentieth century do women become liberated enough to create "a fictional heroine who goes through the process of developing an identity and a self" (7). Just as the male Bildungsroman shows signs of exhaustion, a robust group of rebellious women steps in to re-create the genre in their image. The "female heroine" was "to shatter the mold of the quiescent, unpolitical bourgeois German ideology, where the roots of *Bildung* were to be found" (246). These "rebels and feminists" raise "questions of equality, not only of class, but of sexes" in a way that does not occur in novels by men (251). Thus they rescue a genre that "was believed to be disappearing, even old-fashioned. By breaking into the old genre, the female heroine has brought new meaning to *Bildung* and the *Bildungsroman*" (257-58).

Labovitz, with her image of the vital, iconoclastic heroine contrasts markedly with those critics who emphasize the passive, even self-destructive tendencies of female characters in nineteenth-century fiction. One might well object that Labovitz exhibits a nostalgia for the authentic self that stands in opposition to much postmodern thought. Rita Felski addresses just this problem in her intelligent essay "The Novel of Self-Discovery" (1986). She looks at works of contemporary American and German women writers as leading "to a necessary revision of existing biographical genres such as the *Bildungsroman*" (131). Whereas eighteenth- and nineteenth-century fiction had portrayed women victimized by a hostile society, recent works have transformed women's alienation from society into a positive experience of finding themselves: "The novel of self-discovery is an essentially optimistic genre, reflecting the historical process of women coming to consciousness of female identity as a potentially oppositional force to existing social and cultural values" (132).

This fictional development takes two forms: in "feminine appropriation of the *Bildungsroman*" and in the novels of "awakening" (137). Novels of the first sort portray the gradual process of self-discovery for women. The female protagonist follows a path similar to that of the nineteenth-century male protagonist of the Bildungsroman, although in the case of the modern woman integration into society as a whole is replaced by self-reliance and "the feminist group, the communal household" (137). Yet the new feminist tradition of the Bildungsroman shares important features with its nineteenth-century counterpart: the genre can be defined as biographical, assuming the existence of a coherent self; dialectical, understanding identity to be conditioned by a process of interaction between psychological and social forces; historical, describing identity changing over time; and optimistic, in the belief in a possibility of meaningful development. (138)

Felski associates this variety of the novel of self-discovery with contemporary American fiction; such German women writers as Verena Stefan and Brigitte Schwaiger have produced an alternative type of "novel of awakening," which "traces a process of self-recognition rather than one of development" (141). Felski views this tendency as a neo-romantic feminism, where characters retreat from corrupt patriarchal civilization to rediscover their essential femininity in nature.

By identifying the female Bildungsroman as an essentially optimistic genre that retains a belief in the integrity of the self, Felski realizes that she goes against the grain of much contemporary theory. In response to those feminist critics who stress the liberating power of *l'écriture féminine*, Felski questions "the assumption that the subversion of referentiality and linguistic codes is necessarily revolutionary" (145). As long as women's "access to culture and the media remains an unequal one" the identity of the author still matters (145), and the Bildungsroman can assume "a new function as an articulation of women's new sense of identity and increasing movement into public life" (137). By the same token, the seemingly outmoded search for feminine "essence" in the novels of awakening can serve "as a strategy through which an oppositional and marginalized group can articulate a coherent and fixed identity as the basis for a critique of the problematic features of modernity" (144). In short, one should exercise caution before branding a particular type of novel or criticism regressive. What might seem an outmoded approach to the study of the male Bildungsroman may have liberating potential for the female "novel of self-discovery."

Conclusion

In this study I have sought to trace the history of critical discourse on the Bildungsroman from its inception in the late eighteenth century to the present. As we approach the end of the twentieth century, however, it becomes apparent that we can no longer speak of a single dominant trend in Bildungsroman research. Sociological, psychological, poststructuralist, and feminist studies coexist and compete in a rapidly expanding literature of bewildering diversity, and it becomes increasingly difficult to hear the voice of reason above the din of conflicting opinion. Yet we need not be alarmed, says a reassuring voice, for time will vindicate the perspicacious critic, just as great works of literature endure long after ephemeral publications sink into deserved oblivion.

It is just this faith in the inevitable triumph of a univocal cultural authority that recent criticism of the Bildungsroman challenges. As the history of the genre shows, canon formation proceeds through the deliberate silencing of discord to create the illusion of a coherent tradition. A look at actual literary production around 1800, or at the range of critical opinion that greeted *Wilhelm Meisters Lehrjahre*, reveals a situation far less homogeneous than traditional literary history leads us to assume, one where hierarchies of value no longer seem self-evident. Viewed from this perspective, today's confusion of critical voices represents less a fundamental change from consensus to cacophony than an acceleration of tendencies already present.

The recent diversification of critical opinion is real enough, however, and has its roots in certain changes in the institution of criticism. To cite some of the more obvious factors affecting current scholarship: there are more universities, more students, and more academics than ever before. As a result there are more conferences and journals, and the pressure to publish has increased. Cynics have suggested that the proliferation of critical "isms" in recent years is a direct result of the publish-or-perish syndrome, where young scholars in desperate need of "original" publications crank dusty classics through stylish theories that must be updated with increasing frequency. I would prefer to view the current situation more optimistically, as the emergence of long-suppressed questions of cultural politics, institutional power, and gender relations despite increasingly strident attempts of the political far right to smother dissent.

Taken together, recent developments suggest that Bildungsroman criticism has entered a new phase in its history. Broadly speaking, nineteenth-century critics viewed *Bildung* as an organic process culminating in personal maturity and integration into an affirmed society. This point of view lent itself to first nationalist and then fascist appropriation as the organic theory of the individual became the model for the nation. Opposition to the stress on personal harmony and social affirmation in the Bildungsroman began early with the Romantics, continued among liberal critics of the *Vormärz*, and became the dominant trend in postwar literary criticism. Critics underscored the difficulties attending personal development and the trenchant social criticism often present in the genre. Once again they viewed the Bildungsroman as the German national genre, but one that reveals the disastrous political consequences of quiescence and self-absorption. While this approach has not disappeared altogether, an increasingly international body of critics has begun to address questions typically ignored in previous histories of the genre, and to apply the German term in the study of other national literatures.

As noted in the preface, this export of the Bildungsroman to foreign cultures has provoked indignation among German scholars. Instead of declaring victory for one side or the other in the battle to claim the Bildungsroman, I would argue that there are two different presuppositions at work concerning the genre. The Germanist is likely to insist that the Bildungsroman develops in a particular political and cultural climate in Germany, and that its history in critical discourse remains intimately linked to the shifting fortunes of German history. In contrast, those outside of German studies downplay the national connection and stress the genre's close ties to modernity in general. During the 1930s, for instance, Mikhail Bakhtin identified two features of the Bildungsroman that distinguish it from previous forms of the novel: first, that it depicts a character in the process of becoming, and second, that through the evolving protagonist we glimpse historical change. The Bildungsroman arose during the period that witnessed "the mutation of Order into History" (Foucault 1966, 220), or, rather less grandiosely, at a time when children could expect to grow up into a world that differed significantly from that of their parents (Moretti 1987). In German intellectual history we can locate this transformation in the movement from the Neo-Classicism of Winckelmann and Lessing to Herder's historicism, or at the latest from Friedrich Schlegel's wistful glance back at antiquity in his early essay *Über das Studium der griechischen Poesie* [On the Study of Greek Poetry] (1795-96) to Schiller's embrace of modernity in *Über naive und sentimentalische Dichtung* [On Naive and Sentimental Poetry] (1795-96; on the more "modern" position of Schiller's slightly earlier treatise see Jauß 1970). Seen from a broader perspective, the revolutionary developments in late eighteenth-century German thought mark another chapter in the *Querelle des anciens and des modernes* which began in seventeenth-century France and continues in today's international debates about postmodernism.

Small wonder, then, that the genre that emerged together with modernity should come under renewed scrutiny as modernity gives way to postmodernity. Nineteenth- and early-twentieth-century critics defined the Bildungsroman as a patriarchal, national genre that took pride of place in the new literary canon. Much recent Bildungsroman criticism follows along the lines of the postmodern critique of modernity: it is feminist, international, and questions distinctions between elite and popular fiction in an effort to rehabilitate forgotten works by viewing literature as part of a larger social network. If the Bildungsroman is the genre that portrays historical change, then recent studies of the genre show an interest in new ways of defining that change: in terms of the transformation of the public sphere; the restructuring of the family; and the codification of gender roles, the making of sex. Future studies may well consider depictions of homosexuality in the Bildungsroman or explore its applicability to non-Western cultures. Such expansion of the term by no means invalidates further studies of the historical ties of the Bildungsroman to German culture. By the same token, I doubt that posting critics as border guards will prevent future smugglers from spiriting the genre across national boundaries. In other words, the Bildungsroman will in all likelihood continue to lead a dual life as both the German national genre and the representative genre of modernity.

Works Discussed

Wolfram von Eschenbach. *Parzival.* 1200-1210.

Cervantes Saavedra, Miguel de. *Don Quixote.* 1605-15.

Grimmelshausen, Hans Jakob. *Der abenteuerliche Simplicissimus Teutsch.* 1669.

Schnabel, Johann Gottfried. *Die Insel Felsenburg.* 1731-43.

Richardson, Samuel. *Clarissa.* 1747-48.

Lessing, Gotthold Ephraim. *Miß Sara Sampson.* 1755.

Rousseau, Jean-Jacques. *Julie ou la Nouvelle Héloïse* 1761.

Rousseau, Jean-Jacques. *Emile.* 1762.

Wieland, Christoph Martin. *Geschichte des Agathon.* 1766-67.

LaRoche, Sophie von. *Geschichte des Fräulein von Sternheim.* 1771.

Goethe, Johann Wolfgang. *Die Leiden des jungen Werther.* 1774.

Unger, Friederike Helene. *Julchen Grünthal.* 1784.

Moritz, Karl Philipp. *Anton Reiser.* 1785-1790.

Wobeser, Wilhelmine Karoline von. *Elisa, oder das Weib, wie es seyn sollte.* 1795.

Goethe, Johann Wolfgang. *Wilhelm Meisters Lehrjahre.* 1795-96.

Wolzogen, Karoline von. *Agnes von Lilien.* 1796.

Tieck, Ludwig. *Franz Sternbalds Wanderungen.* 1798.

Schlegel, Friedrich. *Lucinde.* 1799.

Hölderlin, Friedrich. *Hyperion.* 1797-99.

Veit-Schlegel, Dorothea. *Florentin*. 1801.

Novalis (Friedrich von Hardenberg). *Heinrich von Ofterdingen*. 1802.

Jean Paul (Friedrich Richter). *Titan*. 1800-03.

Jean Paul (Friedrich Richter). *Flegeljahre*. 1804-05.

Hegel, Friedrich. *Phänomenologie des Geistes*. 1807.

Eichendorff, Joseph Freiherr von. *Ahnung und Gegenwart*. 1815.

Schopenhauer, Johanna. *Gabriele*. 1819.

Hoffmann, Ernst Theodor Amadeus. *Lebens-Ansichten des Katers Murr*. 1819-21.

Huber, Therese. *Hannah, die Herrnhuterin Deborah Findling*. 1821.

Goethe, Johann Wolfgang. *Wilhelm Meisters Wanderjahre*. 1821-29.

Stendhal. *Vie de Henri Brulard*. 1831-1939.

Immermann, Karl Leberecht. *Die Epigonen*. 1836.

Gotthelf, Jeremias. *Uli der Knecht*. 1841.

Gutzkow, Karl. *Wally die Zweiflerin*. 1843.

Lewald, Fanny. *Jenny*. 1843.

Keller, Gottfried. *Der grüne Heinrich*. 1854-55; 1879-80.

Stifter, Adalbert. *Der Nachsommer*. 1857.

Raabe, Wilhelm. *Der Hungerpastor*. 1864.

Wagner, Richard. *Tristan und Isolde*. 1865.

Marlitt, Eugenie. *Goldelse*. 1866.

Hellern, Wilhelmine von. *Ein Arzt der Seele*. 1869.

Raabe, Wilhelm. *Stopfkuchen*. 1891.

Fontane, Theodor. *Mathilde Möhring*. 1891-1907.

Fontane, Theodor. *Effi Briest*. 1894-95.

Reuter, Gabriele. *Aus guter Familie*. 1895.

Mann, Thomas. *Buddenbrooks*. 1901.

Musil, Robert. *Die Verwirrungen des Zöglings Törleß*. 1906.

Rilke, Rainer Maria. *Die Aufzeichnungen des Malte Laurids Brigge*. 1910.

Mann, Thomas. *Bekenntnisse des Hochstaplers Felix Krull*. 1911-1954.

Mann, Thomas. "Der Tod in Venedig." 1913.

Maugham, Somerset. *Of Human Bondage*. 1915.

Hesse, Hermann. *Demian*. 1919.

Hesse, Hermann. *Siddhartha*. 1922.

Mann, Thomas. *Der Zauberberg*. 1924.

Goebbels, Joseph. *Michael*. 1929.

Musil, Robert. *Der Mann ohne Eigenschaften*. 1930.

Grimm, Hans. *Volk ohne Raum*. 1937.

Hesse, Hermann. *Das Glasperlenspiel*. 1943.

Mann, Thomas. *Doktor Faustus*. 1947.

Grass, Günter. *Die Blechtrommel*. 1959.

Works Cited

Blanckenburg, Friedrich von (1774). *Versuch über den Roman*. Rpt. Stuttgart: Metzler, 1965.

Herder, Johann Gottfried (1774). *Auch eine Philosophie der Geschichte zur Bildung der Menschheit*. Frankfurt: Suhrkamp, 1967.

Schiller, Friedrich (1780). *Versuch über den Zusammenhang der tierischen Natur des Menschen mit seiner Geistigen*. In *Sämtliche Werke*. Munich: Hanser, 1980, 5: 287-324.

Campe, Joachim Heinrich (1782). *Väterlicher Rath für meine Tochter: Ein Gegenstück zum Theophron*. Rpt. Paderborn: Hüttenmann, 1988.

Herder, Johann Gottfried (1784-91). *Ideen zur Philosophie der Geschichte der Menschheit*. 2 vols. Weimar & Berlin: Aufbau, 1965.

Humboldt, Wilhelm von (1792). *Ideen zu einem Versuch die Grenzen der Wirksamkeit des Staats zu bestimmen*. In *Gesammelte Schriften*. Berlin: de Gruyter, 1968, 1: 97-254.

Schiller, Friedrich (1793). *Über Anmut und Würde*. In *Sämtliche Werke*. Munich: Hanser, 1980, 5: 433-88.

Humboldt, Wilhelm von (1794). "Über den Geschlechtsunterschied und dessen Einfluß auf die organische Natur." In *Gesammelte Schriften*. Berlin: de Gruyter, 1968, 1: 311-34.

Schiller, Friedrich (1794-96). Correspondence with Goethe concerning *Wilhelm Meisters Lehrjahre*. Cited from *Goethes Werke*. Hamburg: Wegner, 1950, 8: 521-51.

Humboldt, Wilhelm von (1795). "Über die männliche und weibliche Form." In *Gesammelte Schriften*. Berlin: de Gruyter, 1968, 1: 335-369.

Schiller, Friedrich (1795). *Über die ästhetische Erziehung des Menschen in einer Reihe von Briefen*. In *Sämtliche Werke*. Munich: Hanser, 1980, 5: 570-669.

Schiller, Friedrich (1795-96). *Über naive und sentimentalische Dichtung*. In *Sämtliche Werke*. Munich: Hanser, 1980, 5: 694-780.

Schlegel, Friedrich (1795-96). *Über das Studium der Griechischen Poesie.* In *Kritische Friedrich-Schlegel-Ausgabe*. Ed. Ernst Behler. Vol. 1, *Studien des Klassischen Altertums*. Munich, Paderborn & Vienna: Schöningh, 1979, 217-367.

Goethe, Johann Wolfgang (1796). "Revolutionen" (in *Xenien*). In *Goethes Werke*. Hamburg: Wegner, 1950, 1: 211.

Goethe, Johann Wolfgang (1796a). Letter to Schiller of July 9. Cited from *Goethes Werke*. Hamburg: Wegner, 1950, 8: 542-44.

Körner, Christian Gottfried (1796). Letter to Schiller of November 5 concerning Goethe's *Wilhelm Meisters Lehrjahre*. Cited from *Goethes Werke*. Hamburg: Wegner, 1950, 8: 551-53.

Humboldt, Wilhelm von (1796-97). *Das achtzehnte Jahrhundert*. In *Gesammelte Schriften*. Berlin: de Gruyter, 1968, 2: 1-112.

Schlegel, Friedrich (1798). "Über Goethes Meister." In *Kritische Friedrich-Schlegel-Ausgabe*. Ed. Hans Eichner. Vol. 2, *Charakteristiken und Kritiken* I (1796-1801). Munich, Paderborn & Vienna: Schöningh, 1967, 126-46.

Novalis (Friedrich von Hardenberg) (1798-1800). On Goethe's *Wilhelm Meisters Lehrjahre*. In *Goethes Werke*. Hamburg: Wegner, 1950, 8: 569-71.

Goethe, Johann Wolfgang (1799). "Die Metamorphose der Pflanzen." In *Goethes Werke*. Hamburg: Wegner, 1950, 1: 199-201.

Goethe, Johann Wolfgang (1800). "Natur und Kunst." In *Goethes Werke*. Hamburg: Wegner, 1950, 1: 245.

Goethe, Johann Wolfgang (1811-14). *Aus meinem Leben: Dichtung und Wahrheit*. *Goethes Werke*. Hamburg: Wegner, 1950, 9-10.

Anonymous (1817). "Artikel 'Roman' aus dem *Conversations-Lexicon* von Brockhaus." In Steinecke 1976, 1-14.

Goethe, Johann Wolfgang (1817). "Urworte. Orphisch." In *Goethes Werke*. Hamburg: Wegner, 1950, 1: 359-60.

Morgenstern, Karl (1817). "Über den Geist und Zusammenhang einer Reihe philosophischer Romane." In Selbmann 1988, 45-54.

Goethe, Johann Wolfgang (1820). "Metamorphose der Tiere." In *Goethes Werke*. Hamburg: Wegner, 1950, 1: 201-03.

Morgenstern, Karl (1820). "Ueber das Wesen des Bildungsromans." In Selbmann 1988, 55-72.

Goethe, Johann Wolfgang (1821-29). *Wilhelm Meisters Wanderjahre*. In *Goethes Werke*. Hamburg: Wegner, 1950, 8.

Heine, Heinrich (1822). "Briefe aus Berlin." In Steinecke 1976, 18-19.

Alexis, Willibald (1823). "The Romances of Walter Scott." In Steinecke 1976, 21-35.

Morgenstern, Karl (1824). "Zur Geschichte des Bildungsromans." In Selbmann 1988, 73-99.

Börne, Ludwig (1825). "Cooper's Romane." In Steinecke 1976, 35-38.

Menzel, Wolfgang (1827). "Walter Scott und sein Jahrhundert." In Steinecke 1976, 52-61.

Menzel, Wolfgang (1830). "Romane." In Steinecke 1976, 74-79.

Laube, Heinrich (1833). "Literatur." In Steinecke 1976, 90-94.

Mundt, Theodor (1833). "Ueber Novellenpoesie." In Steinecke 1976, 94-100.

Kühne, Ferdinand Gustav (1835). "Wie die Kunst bei den Deutschen nach Brot geht!" In Steinecke 1976, 119-20.

Wienbarg, Ludolf (1835). "Wanderungen durch den Thierkreis." In Steinecke 1976, 109-116.

Hegel, Georg Wilhelm Friedrich (1835-38). *Vorlesungen über die Ästhetik*. *Sämtliche Werke*. Stuttgart: Frommanns, 1928, 13.

Laube, Heinrich (1836). "Immermann's Epigonen." In Steinecke 1976, 121-25.

Stahr, Adolf (1842). "Der politische Roman." In Steinecke 1976, 162-67.

Auerbach, Berthold (1843). "An J. E. Braun, vom Verfasser der Schwarzwälder Dorfgeschichten." In Steinecke 1976, 170-73.

Prutz, Robert (1845). "Über die Unterhaltungsliteratur, insbesondere der Deutschen." In Steinecke 1976, 205-21.

Schopenhauer, Arthur (1851-60). "Parerga und Paralipomena." In Steinecke 1976, 233-34.

Die Gartenlaube: Beiblatt zum Illustrirten Dorfbarbier. 1 (1853).

Schmidt, Julian (1855). "Weimar und Jena in den Jahren 1794-1806." In Mandelkow 1977, 424-29.

Stifter, Adalbert (1857). *Der Nachsommer*. Rpt. Munich: Winkler, 1987.

Vischer, Friedrich Theodor (1857). *Aesthetik oder Wissenschaft des Schönen*. In Steinecke 1976, 259-69.

Dilthey, Wilhelm (1870). *Leben Schleiermachers*. Rpt. Berlin, Leipzig: de Gruyter, 1922.

Dilthey, Wilhelm (1887). *Die Einbildungskraft des Dichters. Bausteine für eine Poetik*. In Dilthey, *Gesammelte Schriften*. Stuttgart: Teubner, 1958, 6: 103-241.

Driesmans, Heinrich (1904). "Der alte und der neue Erziehungsroman." *Die Gegenwart* 66, No. 42, 247-50.

Dilthey, Wilhelm (1906). *Das Erlebnis und die Dichtung: Lessing, Goethe, Novalis, Hölderlin. Vier Aufsätze*. Rpt. Berlin, Leipzig: Teubner, 1916.

Krüger, Herman Anders (1906). "Der neuere deutsche Bildungsroman." *Westermanns Monatshefte* 51, No. 101, 257-72.

Rehorn, Karl (1906). "Goethe und der moderne Roman." In Mandelkow, 1979, 340-53.

Wundt, Max (1913). *Goethes Wilhelm Meister und die Entwicklung des modernen Lebensideals*. Berlin, Leipzig: de Gruyter.

Ermatinger, Emil (1915-16). *Gottfried Kellers Leben*. Rpt. Zurich: Artemis, 1950.

Mann, Thomas (1916). "Der Entwicklungsroman." In Lämmert 1975, 116-17.

Mann, Thomas (1918). *Betrachtungen eines Unpolitischen*. In *Gesammelte Werke*. Frankfurt am Main: Fischer, 1960, 12: 9-589.

Lukács, Georg (1920). *The Theory of the Novel: A Historico-philosophical Essay on the Forms of Great Epic Literature*. Trans. Anna Bostock. Cambridge: MIT Press, 1971.

Mann, Thomas (1922). "Goethe und Tolstoi." In *Gesammelte Werke*. Frankfurt am Main: Fischer, 1960, 9: 58-173.

Mann, Thomas (1922a). "Von Deutscher Republik." In *Gesammelte Werke*. Frankfurt am Main: Fischer, 1960, 11: 809-52.

Mann, Thomas (1923). "Geist und Wesen der deutschen Republik." In *Gesammelte Werke*. Frankfurt am Main: Fischer, 1960, 11: 853-60.

Mann, Thomas (1924). *Der Zauberberg. Gesammelte Werke*. Frankfurt am Main: Fischer, 1960, 3.

Touaillon, Christine (1925-26). "Bildungsroman." In *Reallexikon der deutschen Literaturgeschichte*. Eds. Paul Merker, Wolfgang Stammler. Berlin: de Gruyter, 1: 141-45.

Gerhard, Melitta (1926). *Der deutsche Entwicklungsroman bis zu Goethes "Wilhelm Meister"*. Rpt. Bern & Munich: Francke, 1968.

Weigand, Hermann J. (1933). *Thomas Mann's Novel "Der Zauberberg"*. New York & London: Appleton-Century.

Stahl, Ernst Ludwig (1934). *Die religiöse und die humanitätsphilosophische Bildungsidee und die Entstehung des deutschen Bildungsromans im 18. Jahrhundert*. Bern: Haupt. Quoted from the partial reprint in Selbmann 1988, 123-81.

Bakhtin, Mikhail (1936-38). "The *Bildungsroman* and Its Significance in the History of Realism (Toward a Historical Typology of the Novel)." In Bakhtin, *Speech Genres & Other Late Essays*. Trans. Vern W. McGee. Eds. Caryl Emerson, Michael Holquist. Austin: University of Texas Press, 1986, 10-59.

Kirsch, Edgar (1937). "Hans Grimms 'Volk ohne Raum' als Bildungsroman." *Dichtung und Volkstum* 38, 475-88.

Kehr, Charlotte (1939). "Der deutsche Entwicklungsroman seit der Jahrhundertwende: Ein Beitrag zur Geschichte des Entwicklungsromans." Leipzig, Phil. Diss.

Mann, Thomas (1939). "Die Kunst des Romans." In *Gesammelte Werke*. Frankfurt am Main: Fischer, 1960, 10: 348-62.

Borcherdt, Hans Heinrich (1941). "Der deutsche Bildungsroman." In Selbmann 1988, 182-238.

Auerbach, Erich (1946). *Mimesis: The Representation of Reality in Western Literature*. Trans. Willard R. Trask. Rpt. Princeton: Princeton University Press, 1968.

Müller, Günther (1948). *Gestaltung-Umgestaltung in Wilhelm Meisters Lehrjahren*. Halle: Niemeyer.

Borcherdt, Hans Heinrich (1949). *Der Roman der Goethezeit*. Stuttgart, Urach: Port.

Schlechta, Karl (1953). *Goethes Wilhelm Meister*. Frankfurt am Main: Klostermann.

Bollnow, Otto Friedrich (1955). "Vorbetrachtungen zum Verständnis der Bildungsidee in Goethes 'Wilhelm Meister.'" *Die Sammlung* 10, 445-463.

Henkel, Arthur (1955). Review of Schlechta 1953. In *Germanisch-Romanische Monatshefte* 36, 85-89.

Wilpert, Gero von (1955). "Bildungsroman." In *Sachwörterbuch der Literatur*. Stuttgart: Kröner.

Pascal, Roy (1956). *The German Novel*. Toronto: University of Toronto Press.

Staiger, Emil (1956). *Goethe*. Vol. 2. Zurich: Artemis.

May, Kurt (1957). "'Wilhelm Meisters Lehrjahre': Ein Bildungsroman?" *Deutsche Vierteljahrsschrift* 31, 1-37.

Borcherdt, Hans Heinrich (1958). "Bildungsroman." In *Reallexikon der deutschen Literaturgeschichte*. 2nd. edition. Berlin: de Gruyter, 1: 175-78.

Heller, Erich (1958). *Thomas Mann: The Ironic German*. Rpt. South Bend, Ind.: Regnery/Gateway, 1979.

Enzensberger, Hans Magnus (1959). "Wilhelm Meister, auf Blech getrommelt." In Loschütz, Gert. *Von Buch zu Buch — Günter Grass in der Kritik: Eine Dokumentation*. Neuwied & Berlin: Luchterhand, 1968, 8-12.

Martini, Fritz (1961). "Der Bildungsroman: Zur Geschichte des Wortes und der Theorie." *Deutsche Vierteljahrsschrift* 35, 44-63. Cited from Selbmann 1988, 239-64. Trans. in Hardin 1991, 1-25.

Lukács, Georg (1962). "Preface." In Lukács 1920, 11-23.

Martini, Fritz (1962). *Deutsche Literatur im bürgerlichen Realismus 1848-1898*. Rpt. Stuttgart: Metzler, 1974.

Hass, Hans-Egon (1963). "Wilhelm Meisters Lehrjahre." In *Der deutsche Roman: Vom Barock bis zur Gegenwart*. Ed. Benno von Wiese. Düsseldorf: Bagel, 1:132-210.

Killy, Walther (1963). "Utopische Gegenwart. Stifter: 'Der Nachsommer.'" In his *Romane des 19. Jahrhunderts: Wirklichkeit und Kunstcharakter*. Rpt. Göttingen: Vandenhoeck & Ruprecht, 1967, 83-103.

Lange, Victor (1963). "Stifter: Der Nachsommer." In *Der deutsche Roman: Vom Barock bis zur Gegenwart. Struktur und Geschichte.* Ed. Benno von Wiese. Düsseldorf: Bagel, 2: 34-75.

Preisendanz, Wolfgang (1963). "Keller: Der grüne Heinrich." In *Der deutsche Roman: Vom Barock bis zur Gegenwart. Struktur und Geschichte.* Ed. Benno von Wiese. Düsseldorf: Bagel, 2: 76-127.

Glaser, Horst Albert (1965). *Die Restauration des Schönen: Stifters "Nachsommer."* Stuttgart: Metzler.

Lämmert, Eberhard (1965). "Nachwort." In Blanckenburg 1774, 543-83.

Ryan, Lawrence (1965). *Hölderlins 'Hyperion': Exzentrische Bahn und Dichterberuf.* Stuttgart: Metzler.

Blumenberg, Hans (1966). *The Legitimacy of the Modern Age.* Trans. Robert A. Wallace. Cambridge Mass. & London: MIT Press.

Eichner, Hans (1966). "Zur Deutung von 'Wilhelm Meisters Lehrjahren.'" *Jahrbuch des freien deutschen Hochstifts*, 165-196.

Foucault, Michel (1966). *The Order of Things: An Archaeology of the Human Sciences.* Trans. New York: Vintage, 1973.

Eichner, Hans (1967). "Einleitung." In Friedrich Schlegel (1798), ix-cv.

Hoffmann, Werner (1967). "Grimmelshausens 'Simplizissimus': Nicht doch ein Bildungsroman?" *Germanisch-Romanische Monatshefte* 48, 166-80.

Scharfschwerdt, Jürgen (1967). *Thomas Mann und der deutsche Bildungsroman: Eine Untersuchung zu den Problemen einer literarischen Tradition.* Stuttgart, Berlin, Cologne & Mainz: Kohlhammer.

Köhn, Lothar (1968). *Entwicklungs- und Bildungsroman: Ein Forschungsbericht. Erweiterter Sonderdruck aus Deutsche Vierteljahrsschrift für Literaturwissenschaft* 42, Nos. 3-4. Stuttgart: Metzler, 1969. Abbreviated version in Selbmann 1988, 291-373.

Röder, Gerda (1968). *Glück und glückliches Ende im deutschen Bildungsroman: Eine Studie zu Goethes "Wilhelm Meister."* Munich: Heuber, 1968.

Jost, François (1969). "La Tradition du *Bildungsroman*." *Comparative Literature* 21, 97-115.

Cunliffe, W. Gordon (1969). *Günter Grass*. New York: Twayne.

Laufhütte, Hartmut (1969). *Wirklichkeit und Kunst in Gottfried Kellers Roman "Der grüne Heinrich."* Bonn: Bouvier.

Ziolkowski, Theodore (1969). *Dimensions of the Modern Novel: German Texts and European Contexts*. Princeton: Princeton University Press.

Jauß, Hans Robert (1970). "Schlegels und Schillers Replik auf die 'Querelle des Anciens et des Modernes.'" In Jauß, *Literaturgeschichte als Provokation*. Frankfurt am Main: Suhrkamp, 67-106.

Abrams, M. H. (1971). *Natural Supernaturalism: Tradition and Revolution in Romantic Literature*. New York & London: Norton.

Gille, Klaus Friedrich (1971). *"Wilhelm Meister" im Urteil der Zeitgenossen: Ein Beitrag zur Wirkungsgeschichte Goethes*. Leiden: van Gorcum.

Lämmert, Eberhard, ed. (1971). *Romantheorie: Dokumentation ihrer Geschichte in Deutschland 1620-1880*. Berlin & Cologne: Kiepenheuer & Witsch.

Lichtenstein, E. (1971). "Bildung." In *Historisches Wörterbuch der Philosophie*. Vol. 1. Basel & Stuttgart: Schwabe, 921-37.

Trommler, Frank (1971). "Von Stalin zu Hölderlin: Über den Entwicklungsroman in der DDR." *Basis* 2, 141-90.

Jacobs, Jürgen (1972). *Wilhelm Meister und seine Brüder: Untersuchungen zum deutschen Bildungsroman*. Munich: Fink.

Just, Georg (1972). *Darstellung und Appell in der "Blechtrommel" von Günter Grass: Darstellungsästhetik versus Wirkungsästhetik*. Frankfurt am Main: Athenäum.

Peschken, Bernd (1972). *Versuch einer germanistichen Ideologiekritik: Goethe, Lessing, Novalis, Tieck, Hölderlin, Heine in Wilhelm Diltheys und Julian Schmidts Vorstellungen*. Stuttgart: Metzler.

Vierhaus, Rudolf (1972). "Bildung." In *Geschichtliche Grundbegriffe: Historisches Lexikon zur politisch-sozialen Sprache in Deutschland*. Vol. 1. Stuttgart: Klett, 508-51.

Schlaffer, Heinz (1973). *Der Bürger als Held: Sozialgeschichtliche Auflösungen literarischer Widersprüche*. Edition Suhrkamp 624. Frankfurt am Main: Suhrkamp.

Buckley, Jerome Hamilton (1974). *Season of Youth: The Bildungsroman from Dickens to Golding*. Cambridge: Harvard University Press.

Engelsing, Rolf (1974). *Der Bürger als Leser: Lesergeschichte in Deutschland 1500-1800*. Stuttgart: Metzler.

Mayer, Gerhart (1974). "Zum deutschen Antibildungsroman." *Jahrbuch der Raabe-Gesellschaft*, 41-64.

Miles, David H. (1974). "The Picaro's Journey to the Confessional: The Changing Image of the Hero in the German Bildungsroman." *PMLA* 89, 980-92.

Reed, T. J. (1974). *Thomas Mann: The Uses of Tradition*. Oxford: Clarendon Press.

Baioni, Giuliano (1975). "Märchen — Wilhelm Meisters Lehrjahre — Hermann und Dorothea: Zur Gesellschaftsidee der deutschen Klassik." *Goethe Jahrbuch* 92, 73-127.

Bruford, W. H. (1975). *The German Tradition of Self-Cultivation: "Bildung" from Humboldt to Thomas Mann*. Cambridge: Cambridge University Press.

Janz, Rolf-Peter (1975). "Zum sozialen Gehalt der *Lehrjahre*." In *Literaturwissenschaft und Geschichtsphilosophie: Festschrift für Wilhelm Emrich*. Berlin & New York: de Gruyter, 320-40.

Lämmert, Eberhard, ed. (1975). *Romantheorie: Dokumentation ihrer Geschichte in Deutschland seit 1880*. Cologne: Kiepenheuer & Witsch.

Schrader, Monika (1975). *Mimesis und Poiesis: Poetologische Studien zum Bildungsroman*. Berlin & New York: de Gruyter.

Steinecke, Hartmut (1975). *Romantheorie und Romankritik in Deutschland: Die Entwicklung des Gattungsverständnisses von der Scott-Rezeption bis zum programmatischen Realismus.* Vol. 1. Stuttgart: Metzler.

Steinecke, Hartmut (1976). *Romantheorie und Romankritik in Deutschland.* Vol. 2, *Quellen.* Stuttgart: Metzler.

Berger, Albert (1977). *Ästhetik und Bildungsroman: Goethes "Wilhelm Meisters Lehrjahre."* Vienna: Braumüller.

Foucault, Michel (1977). "What is an Author?" In *Language, Counter-Memory, Practice: Selected Essays and Interviews.* Ed. Donald F. Bouchard. Trans. Bouchard and Sherry Simon. Ithaca, N. Y.: Cornell University Press, 113-38.

Thomas, R. Hinton (1977). "The Uses of 'Bildung.'" *German Life and Letters* 30, 177-86.

Mandelkow, Karl Robert, ed. (1977). *Goethe im Urteil seiner Kritiker: Dokumente zur Wirkungsgeschichte Goethes in Deutschland.* Vol. 2, 1832-1870. Munich: Beck.

Muschg, Adolf (1977). *Gottfried Keller.* Munich: Kindler.

Voßkamp, Wilhelm (1977). "Gattungen als literarisch-soziale Institutionen." In *Textsortenlehre-Gattungsgeschichte.* Ed. Walter Hinck. Heidelberg: Quelle & Meyer, 27-44.

Cocalis, Susan L. (1978). "The Transformation of Bildung from an Image to an Ideal." *Monatshefte* 70, 399-414.

Kittler, Friedrich A. (1978). "Über die Sozialisation Wilhelm Meisters." In Gerhard Kaiser and Friedrich A. Kittler. *Dichtung als Sozialisationsspiel: Studien zu Goethe und Gottfried Keller.* Göttingen: Vandenhoeck & Ruprecht.

Schlaffer, Heinz (1978). "Exoterik und Esoterik in Goethes Romanen." *Goethe Jahrbuch* 95, 212-226.

Swales, Martin (1978). *The German Bildungsroman from Wieland to Hesse.* Princeton: Princeton University Press.

Swales, Martin (1978a). "Irony and the Novel: Reflections on the German Bildungsroman." In Hardin 1991, 46-68.

Becker-Cantarino, Barbara (1979). "Priesterin und Lichtbringerin: Zur Ideologie des weiblichen Charakters in der Frühromantik." In Paulsen, ed., 111-24.

Bovenschen, Silvia (1979). *Die imaginierte Weiblichkeit: Exemplarische Untersuchungen zu kulturgeschichtlichen und literarischen Präsentationsformen des Weiblichen.* Frankfurt am Main: Suhrkamp.

Köpke, Wulf (1979). "Die emanzipierte Frau in der Goethezeit und ihre Darstellung in der Literatur." In Paulsen, ed., 96-110.

Neuhaus, Volker (1979). *Günter Grass.* Stuttgart: Metzler.

Paulsen, Wolfgang, ed. (1979). *Die Frau als Heldin und Autorin: Neue kritische Ansätze zur deutschen Literatur.* Bern & Munich: Francke.

Foucault, Michel (1979). *Discipline and Punish: The Birth of the Prison.* Trans. Alan Sheridan. New York, Vintage.

Mandelkow, Karl Robert, ed. (1979). *Goethe im Urteil seiner Kritiker: Dokumente zur Wirkungsgeschichte Goethes in Deutschland.* Vol. 3, 1870-1918. Munich: Beck.

Miles, David H. (1979). "Portrait of the Marxist as a Young Hegelian: Lukács' *Theory of the Novel.*" *PMLA* 94, 22-35.

Witte, W. (1979-80). "Alien Corn: The 'Bildungsroman': Not for Export?" *German Life and Letters* 33, 87-96.

Janz, Rolf-Peter (1980). "Bildungsroman." In *Deutsche Literatur: Eine Sozialgeschichte.* Vol. 5. Ed. Horst Albert Glaser. Reinbek, Rowohlt, 144-63.

Ketelsen, Uwe-K. (1980). "Adalbert Stifter: Der Nachsommer. Die Vernichtung der historischen Realität in der Ästhetisierung des bürgerlichen Alltags." In *Romane und Erzählungen des Bürgerlichen Realismus: Neue Interpretationen.* Ed. Horst Denkler. Stuttgart: Reclam, 188-202.

Mandelkow, Karl Robert (1980). *Goethe in Deutschland: Rezeptionsgeschichte eines Klassikers.* Vol. 1, 1773-1918. Munich: Beck.

Roberts, David (1980). *The Indirections of Desire: Hamlet in Goethes "Wilhelm Meister."* Heidelberg: Winter.

Sautermeister, Gert (1980). "Der grüne Heinrich: Gesellschaftsroman, Seelendrama, Romankunst." In *Romane und Erzählungen des Bürgerlichen Realismus: Neue Interpretationen.* Ed. Horst Denkler. Stuttgart: Reclam, 80-123.

Sammons, Jeffrey L. (1981). "The Mystery of the Missing *Bildungsroman*, or: What Happened to Wilhelm Meister's Legacy?" *Genre* 14, 229-246.

Kaiser, Gerhard (1981). *Gottfried Keller: Das gedichtete Leben.* Frankfurt am Main: Insel.

Selbmann, Rolf (1981). *Theater im Roman: Studien zum Strukturwandel des deutschen Bildungsromans.* Munich: Fink.

Beddow, Michael (1982). *The Fiction of Humanity: Studies in the Bildungsroman from Wieland to Thomas Mann.* Cambridge: Cambridge University Press.

Blackwell, Jeannine (1982). "*Bildungsroman mit Dame:* The Heroine in the German Bildungsroman from 1770 to 1900." Diss. Indiana University.

Bürger, Christa (1982). "Einleitung: Die Dichotomie von hoher und niederer Literatur. Eine Problemskizze." In *Zur Dichotomisierung von hoher und niederer Literatur.* Eds. C. Bürger, P. Bürger and J. Schulte-Sasse. Frankfurt am Main: Suhrkamp, 9-39.

Germer, Helmut (1982). *The German Novel of Education from 1764 to 1792: A Complete Bibliography and Analysis.* German Language and Literature 550. Bern & Frankfurt am Main: Lang.

Martin, Elaine (1982). "Theoretical Soundings: The Female Archetypal Quest in Contemporary French and German Women's Fiction." *Perspectives on Contemporary Literature* 8, 48-57.

Sagmo, Ivar (1982). *Bildungsroman und Geschichtsphilosophie: Eine Studie zu Goethes Roman "Wilhelm Meisters Lehrjahre."* Bonn: Bouvier.

Swales, Martin (1982). "Utopie und Bildungsroman." In Vosskamp, (1982), 218-26.

Voßkamp, Wilhelm (1982). "Utopie und Utopiekritik in Goethes Romanen *Wilhelm Meisters Lehrjahre* und *Wilhelm Meisters Wanderjahre.*" In Vosskamp, ed. *Utopieforschung: Interdisziplinäre Studien zur neuzeitlichen Utopie.* Stuttgart: Metzler, 3: 227-49.

Abel, Elizabeth, Marianne Hirsch, and Elizabeth Langland (1983). "Introduction." In *The Voyage In: Fictions of Female Development.* Eds. Abel, Hirsch, Langland. Hanover N. H. & London: University Press of New England, 3-19.

Esselborn-Krumbiegel, Helga (1983). *Der "Held" im Roman: Formen des deutschen Entwicklungsromans im frühen 20. Jahrhundert.* Impulse der Forschung 39. Darmstadt: Wissenschaftliche Buchgesellschaft.

Hirsch, Marianne (1983). "Spiritual *Bildung*: The Beautiful Soul as Paradigm." In Abel et al. 1983, 23-48.

Hörisch, Jochen (1983). *Gott, Geld und Glück: Zur Logik der Liebe in den Bildungsromanen Goethes, Kellers und Thomas Manns.* Frankfurt am Main: Suhrkamp.

Meise, Helga (1983). *Die Unschuld und die Schrift: Deutsche Frauenromane im 18. Jahrhundert.* Reihe Métro 14. Berlin & Marburg: Guttandin & Hoppe.

Müller-Seidel, Walter (1983). "Naturforschung und Deutsche Klassik: Die Jenaer Gespräche im Juli 1794." In his *Die Geschichtlichkeit der deutschen Klassik: Literatur und Denkformen um 1800.* Stuttgart: Metzler, 105-118.

Minden, Michael (1983). "The Place of Inheritance in the Bildungsroman: *Agathon*, *Wilhelm Meisters Lehrjahre*, and *Der Nachsommer.*" Cited from Hardin 1991, 254-92.

Sorg, Klaus-Dieter (1983). *Gebrochene Teleologie: Studien zum Bildungsroman von Goethe bis Thomas Mann.* Heidelberg: Winter.

Voris, Renate (1983). "Biographie — Roman — Autobiographie: Adolf Muschgs *Gottfried Keller*." *Jahrbuch der deutschen Schillergesellschaft* 27, 283-302.

Holub, Robert C. (1984). *Reception Theory: A Critical Introduction*. London & New York: Methuen.

Laufhütte, Hartmut (1984). "Gottfried Keller: 'Der grüne Heinrich.' Zur Problematik literaturwissenschaftlicher Aktualisierung." In *Zu Gottfried Keller*. Ed. Hartmut Steinecke. Stuttgart: Klett, 18-39.

Schings, Hans-Jürgen (1984). "Agathon, Anton Reiser, Wilhelm Meister: Zur Pathogenese des modernen Subjekts im Bildungsroman." In *Goethe im Kontext*. Ed. Wolfgang Wittkowski. Tübingen: Niemeyer, 42-68.

Selbmann, Rolf (1984). *Der deutsche Bildungsroman*. Sammlung Metzler 214. Stuttgart: Metzler.

Shaffner, Randolph P. (1984). *The Apprenticeship Novel: A Study of the "Bildungsroman" as a Regulative Type in Western Literature with a Focus on Three Classic Representatives by Goethe, Maugham, and Mann*. New York, Bern & Frankfurt am Main: Lange.

Steinecke, Hartmut (1984). "*Wilhelm Meister* und die Folgen: Goethes Roman und die Entwicklung der Gattung im 19. Jahrhundert." In *Goethe im Kontext*. Ed. Wolfgang Wittkowski. Tübingen: Niemeyer, 89-118.

Böhm, Karl Werner (1985). "Die homosexuellen Elemente in Thomas Manns 'Der Zauberberg.'" In *Stationen der Thomas-Mann-Forschung: Aufsätze seit 1970*. Ed. Hermann Kurzke. Würzburg: Königshausen + Neumann, 145-65.

Heuser, Magdalene (1985). "'Spuren trauriger Selbstvergessenheit': Möglichkeiten eines weiblichen Bildungsromans um 1800: Friederike Helene Unger.'" In *Frauensprache-Frauenliteratur/Für und Wider einer Psychoanalyse literarischer Texte*. Vol. 6 of *Kontroversen, alte und neue*. Akten des VII. Internationalen Germanisten-Kongresses Göttingen, 30-42.

Kittler, Friedrich A. (1985). *Aufschreibesysteme 1800/1900*. Munich: Fink. Translated by Chris Cullens and Michael Metteer as *Discourse Networks 1800/1900*. Stanford: Stanford University Press, 1990.

Showalter, Elaine (1985). "Introduction: The Feminist Critical Revolution." In *Feminist Criticism: Essays on Women, Literature Theory*. Ed. Elaine Showalter. New York: Pantheon, 3-17.

Schweitzer, Antonie and Simone Sitte (1985). "Tugend — Opfer — Rebellion: Zum Bild der Frau im weiblichen Erziehungs- und Bildungsroman." In *Frauen Literatur Geschichte: Schreibende Frauen vom Mittelalter bis zur Gegenwart*. Eds. Hiltrud Gnüg and Renate Möhrmann. Stuttgart: Metzler, 144-65.

Corngold, Stanley (1986). *The Fate of the Self: German Writers and French Theory*. New York: Columbia University Press.

Engelhardt, Ulrich (1986). *"Bildungsbürgertum": Begriffs- und Dogmengeschichte eines Etiketts*. Stuttgart: Klett.

Felski, Rita (1986). "The Novel of Self-Discovery: A Necessary Fiction?" *Southern Review* 19, 131-48.

Holquist, Michael (1986). "Introduction." In Bakhtin 1936-38, ix-xxiii.

Krumme, Detlef (1986). *Günter Grass: Die Blechtrommel*. Munich, Vienna: Hanser.

Labovitz, Esther Kleinbord (1986). *The Myth of the Heroine: The Female 'Bildungsroman' in the Twentieth Century*. Second Edition. New York, Bern & Frankfurt am Main: Lang, 1988.

Zantop, Susanne (1986). "Eignes Selbst und fremde Formen: Goethes 'Bekenntnisse einer schönen Seele.'" *Goethe Yearbook* 3, 73-92.

Amrine, Frederick (1987). "Rethinking the *Bildungsroman*." *Michigan Germanic Studies* 13, 119-39.

Moretti, Franco (1987). *The Way of the World: The Bildungsroman in European Culture*. London: Verso.

Smith, John H. (1987). "Sexual Difference, *Bildung*, and the *Bildungsroman*." *Michigan Germanic Studies* 13, 206-25.

132   *The German Bildungsroman*

Steinecke, Hartmut (1987). *Romanpoetik von Goethe bis Thomas Mann: Entwicklungen und Probleme der "demokratischen Kunstform" in Deutschland.* Munich: Fink.

Weissberg, Liliane (1987). "The Master's Theme, and Some Variations: Dorothea Schlegel's *Florentin* as *Bildungsroman.*" *Michigan Germanic Studies* 13, 169-81.

Berman, Russell A. (1988). "Literary Criticism from Empire to Dictatorship, 1870-1933." In Hohendahl 1988, 277-357.

Hohendahl, Peter Uwe (1988). "Literary Criticism in the Epoch of Liberalism, 1820-70." In Hohendahl ed. *A History of German Literary Criticism, 1730-1980.* Lincoln & London: University of Nebraska Press, 179-276.

Mahoney, Dennis F. (1988). *Der Roman der Goethezeit (1774-1829).* Sammlung Metzler 241. Stuttgart: Metzler.

Ratz, Norbert (1988). *Der Identitätsroman: Eine Strukturanalyse.* Untersuchungen zur deutschen Literaturgeschichte 44. Tübingen: Niemeyer.

Selbmann, Rolf, ed. (1988). *Zur Geschichte des deutschen Bildungsromans.* Wege der Forschung 640. Darmstadt: Wissenschaftliche Buchgesellschaft.

Hohendahl, Peter Uwe (1989). *Building a National Literature: The Case of Germany 1830-1870.* Trans. Renate Baron Franciscono. Ithaca, N. Y. & London: Cornell University Press.

Jacobs, Jürgen and Markus Krause (1989). *Der deutsche Bildungsroman: Gattungsgeschichte vom 18. bis zum 20. Jahrhundert.* Arbeitsbücher zur Literaturgeschichte. Eds. Wilfried Barner and Gunter E. Grimm. Munich: Beck.

Mandelkow, Karl Robert (1989). *Goethe in Deutschland: Rezeptionsgeschichte eines Klassikers.* Vol. 2, 1919-1982. Munich: Beck.

Bürger, Christa (1990). *Leben Schreiben: Die Klassik, die Romantik und der Ort der Frauen.* Stuttgart: Metzler.

Fuderer, Laura Sue (1990). *The Female Bildungsroman in English: An Annotated Bibliography of Criticism.* New York: MLA.

Laqueur, Thomas (1990). *Making Sex: Body and Gender from the Greeks to Freud*. Cambridge, Mass. & London: Harvard University Press.

Wellbery, David E. (1990). "Foreword." In Kittler 1985, vii-xxxiii.

Hardin, James N., ed. (1991). *Reflection and Action: Essays on the Bildungsroman*. Columbia: University of South Carolina Press.

Mahoney, Dennis F. (1991). "The Apprenticeship of the Reader: The Bildungsroman of the 'Age of Goethe.'" In Hardin 1991, 97-117.

Mücke, Dorothea E. von (1991). *Virtue and the Veil of Illusion: Generic Innovation and the Pedagogical Project in Eighteenth-Century Literature*. Stanford: Stanford University Press.

Sammons, Jeffrey L. (1991). "The Bildungsroman for Nonspecialists: An Attempt at a Clarification." In Hardin 1991, 26-45.

Steinecke, Hartmut (1991). *Deutschsprachige Romane 1815-1830 in der Fürstlichen Bibliothek Corvey: Probleme der Erforschung — Bestandsverzeichnis*. Stuttgart: Belser.

Kontje, Todd (1992). *Private Lives in the Public Sphere: The German "Bildungsroman" as Metafiction*. University Park, Pa.: Penn State Press.

Mayer, Gerhart (1992). *Der deutsche Bildungsroman: Von der Aufklärung bis zur Gegenwart*. Stuttgart: Metzler.

Tobin, Robert (1993). "Healthy Families: Medicine, Patriarchy, and Heterosexuality in 18th-Century German Novels." In *Impure Reason: Dialectic of Enlightenment in Germany*. Eds. W. Daniel Wilson and Robert C. Holub. Detroit: Wayne State University Press, forthcoming.

Index